Native Americans of the Great Lakes

Titles in the Indigenous Peoples of North America Series Include:

Native Americans of the Great Lakes

Stuart A. Kallen

Lucent Books, Inc.
P.O. Box 289011, San Diego, California

Library of Congress Cataloging-in-Publication Data

Kallen, Stuart A., 1955–
　　Native Americans of the Great Lakes / by Stuart A. Kallen.
　　　　p.　　cm. — (Indigenous peoples of North America)
　　Includes bibliographical references and index.
　　Summary: Discusses the history, daily lives, culture, religion, and
conflicts of the Indians that lived in the Great Lakes region, including
the various Iroquois and Algonquian peoples.
　　ISBN 1-56006-568-0 (lib. : alk. paper)
　　1. Indians of North America—Great Lakes—History Juvenile
literature.　2. Indians of North America—Great Lakes—Social life
and customs Juvenile literature.　[1. Indians of North America—Great
Lakes.]　I. Title.　II. Series.
E78.G7K35　2000
977.004'97—dc21　　　　　　　　　　　　　　　　　　　　99-23523
　　　　　　　　　　　　　　　　　　　　　　　　　　　　　　CIP

Copyright 2000 by Lucent Books, Inc.
P.O. Box 289011, San Diego, California 92198-9011

Printed in the U.S.A.

Contents

Foreword

North America's native peoples are often relegated to history—viewed primarily as remnants of another era—or cast in the stereotypical images long found in popular entertainment and even literature. Efforts to characterize Native Americans typically result in idealized portrayals of spiritualists communing with nature or bigoted descriptions of savages incapable of living in civilized society. Lost in these unfortunate images is the rich variety of customs, beliefs, and values that comprised—and still comprise—many of North America's native populations.

The *Indigenous Peoples of North America* series strives to present a complex, realistic picture of the many and varied Native American cultures. Each book in the series offers historical perspectives as well as a view of contemporary life of individual tribes and tribes that share a common region. The series examines traditional family life, spirituality, interaction with other native and non-native peoples, warfare, and the ways the environment shaped the lives and cultures of North America's indigenous populations. Each book ends with a discussion of life today for the Native Americans of a given region or tribe.

In any discussion of the Native American experience, there are bound to be sim-

ilarities. All tribes share a past filled with unceasing white expansion and resistance that led to more than four hundred years of conflict. One U.S. administration after another pursued this goal and fought Indians who attempted to defend their homelands and ways of life. Although no war was ever formally declared, the U.S. policy of conquest precluded any chance of white and Native American peoples living together peacefully. Between 1780 and 1890, Americans killed hundreds of thousands of Indians and wiped out whole tribes.

The Indians lost the fight for their land and ways of life, though not for lack of bravery, skill, or a sense of purpose. They simply could not contend with the overwhelming numbers of whites arriving from Europe or the superior weapons they brought with them. Lack of unity also contributed to the defeat of the Native Americans. For most, tribal identity was more important than racial identity. This loyalty left the Indians at a distinct disadvantage. Whites had a strong racial identity and they fought alongside each other even when there was disagreement because they shared a racial destiny.

Although all Native Americans share this tragic history they have many distinct differences. For example, some tribes and individuals sought to cooperate almost immediately with the U.S. government while others steadfastly resisted the white presence. Life before the arrival of white settlers also varied. The nomads of the Plains developed altogether different lifestyles and customs from the fishermen of the Northwest coast.

Contemporary life is no different in this regard. Many Native Americans—forced onto reservations by the American government—struggle with poverty, poor health, and inferior schooling. But others have regained a sense of pride in themselves and their heritage, enabling them to search out new routes to self-sufficiency and prosperity.

The *Indigenous Peoples of North America* series attempts to capture the differences as well as similarities that make up the experiences of North America's native populations—both past and present. Fully documented primary and secondary source quotations enliven the text. Sidebars highlight events, personalities, and traditions. Bibliographies provide readers with ideas for further research. In all, each book in this dynamic series provides students with a wealth of information as well as launching points for further research.

An Ancient Odyssey

The Great Lakes region of the United States and Canada stretches almost 750 miles from east to west and 500 miles from north to south. This region is one of the most industrialized areas in the world. Steel mills, automobile factories, and chemical plants line the shores of the Great Lakes. Populous cities like Buffalo, Cleveland, Toronto, Detroit, Chicago, and Milwaukee are among the world's major manufacturing centers. Of the tens of millions of people who live around the Great Lakes, the majority are descendants of European Americans, African Americans, and Latin Americans.

But interspersed between the factories, skyscrapers, and strip malls are lands where North America's indigenous, or original, inhabitants still reside. These are men, women, and children whose ancestry dates back to Native American tribes of the Iroquois, Seneca, Mohawk, Ojibwa, Illinois, Menominee, Ottawa, and others. Some of these Native Americans live on reservations while others live in the towns and cities that dot the landscape.

The people of these tribes have a rich history in the region that dates back over ten thousand years. When the first Europeans arrived in the Great Lakes region in the early seventeenth century, Native Americans had their own thriving civilization there, which included a culture rich in religion, self-government, and history. They were farmers, hunters, politicians, warriors, artisans, healers, and more.

Since the Native Americans did not have a written language, most of what has been written about the tribes throughout the centuries was filtered through the eyes of white people. Europeans looked upon the Native Americans as primitive "Stone Age" people and many called them "savages," "barbarians," and "heathens." While recording how the Native Americans lived, many European writers misunderstood or exaggerated aspects of Native American culture. This bias perpetuated many myths in American society about the people of the lakes.

In his 1933 book *Land of the Spotted Eagle,* Lakota Indian Luther Standing Bear commented on the white bias against Native Americans in books at that time:

> Irreparable damage had been done by white writers who discredit the Indian. Books have been written of the native American, so distorting his true nature that he scarcely resembles the real man; his faults have been magnified and his virtues minimized. . . . Books, paintings, and pictures have all joined in glorifying the pioneer—the hunter, trapper, woodsman, cowboy, and soldiery—in their course of conquest across the country, a conquest that could only have been realized by committing untold offenses against the aboriginal people. But who proclaims that every battle by the American Indian was a holy fight for the protection of wives, little children, and homeland; that every "massacre" was the frenzied expression of the right to exist?[1]

The first Europeans in the Great Lakes region were French explorers and fur

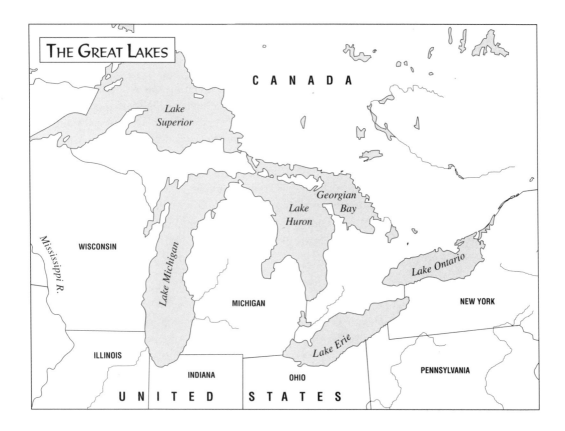

THE GREAT LAKES

CANADA

Lake Superior

Georgian Bay

Lake Huron

Mississippi R.

WISCONSIN

Lake Michigan

Lake Ontario

MICHIGAN

NEW YORK

ILLINOIS

Lake Erie

INDIANA

OHIO

PENNSYLVANIA

UNITED STATES

traders who introduced guns, iron, the wheel, and manufactured goods to the natives. They also brought a host of deadly diseases to which Native Americans had little resistance, including smallpox, measles, and cholera. These outbreaks killed one-third to one-half or more of a native population whenever they occurred.

Migrants from Great Britain, Germany, and Scandinavia later settled in the region, pushing the surviving Native Americans off their ancestral homelands and forcing them onto reservations. By the twentieth century many of the people who had once thrived in the forests of the Great Lakes region were reduced to living in poverty and subsisting on what little the U.S. government provided in the form of welfare, unemployment benefits, and subsidies.

Maintaining Tribal Traditions

Although the past three hundred years have not been kind to the Native Americans in the Great Lakes region, other Americans are coming to terms with Native American history and culture. In a booklet called *We, the First Americans,* published by the U.S. Department of Census, author Edna L. Paisano writes,

The Great Lakes

Five lakes, Superior, Michigan, Huron, Erie, and Ontario, make up the body of water collectively known as the Great Lakes. Lake St. Clair, although not considered a "Great" lake is also part of this larger system. They are located in east central North America at the border between Canada and the United States. The states that border the lakes are New York, Pennsylvania, Ohio, Michigan, Indiana, Illinois, Wisconsin, and Minnesota. The Canadian province of Ontario borders the northern shores of four of the five Great Lakes, excluding only Lake Michigan.

With a combined area of 94,950 square miles, the Great Lakes are the world's largest body of fresh water. They were created by the scouring of Ice Age glaciers, the last of which melted and retreated approximately eighteen thousand years ago.

Many names of cities, towns, and states in the region—and two of the Great Lakes themselves, Huron and Erie—were named after Native American tribes. States (regardless of their location) whose names derived from Great Lakes tribes include Illinois, Iowa, and North and South Dakota. Dozens of cities were named after tribes, including Seneca Falls, New York; Miami, Ohio; Muncie, Indiana; and the three Wisconsin cities of Kickapoo, Menominee, and Winnebago. Other Native American tribes that have contributed names in the Great Lakes region include the Cayuga, Ottawa, Mohawk, Ojibwa, Oneida, Onondaga, Tuscarora, and Shawnee.

Europeans introduced guns, iron, the wheel, and other manufactured goods to the Native Americans.

We, the American Indians . . . are the original inhabitants of America. Our land once was a vast stretch of forest, plains, and mountains extending from the Atlantic to the Pacific Ocean and from the Arctic Circle to the tip of South America. In many American Indian . . . lands across the country, we still hunt, fish, and gather from the land, rivers, and seas, much as we have for thousands of years.

Our long and proud heritage continues in our many traditional foods, medicines, and names all Americans use. We have survived numerous disruptions of our lives and dislocations from our native habitats. Today, while still maintaining our tribal traditions and languages, we strive to accept new technologies which address our needs.[2]

Native Americans of the Great Lakes have greatly influenced the growth and prosperity of the United States and Canada since the first Europeans arrived in the 1600s. Today, the Native Americans continue to influence people and their governments by way of hundreds of websites on the Internet and with a newly found political influence in city, state, and federal governments.

Chapter 1

Native Peoples of the Great Lakes

The Native Americans who originated in the Great Lakes region survived for centuries in a harsh physical environment. The rugged land was formed eons ago by glaciers, and even today much of the area is enveloped by a wintry mix of snow and ice for up to six months of every year.

The Great Lakes were formed at the end of the last Ice Age, about ten thousand years ago, when glaciers melted and receded far to the north. The melting mass of ice left behind depressions in the landscape that quickly filled with cold, clear waters. The shores of the lakes were surrounded by grassy marshes that attracted mammoths, mastodons, caribou, and other large mammals. This, in turn, lured to the area the first humans—whom anthropologists believe crossed into the North American continent from Siberia during the last Ice Age.

Over the centuries the earth's climate warmed, and the terrain in the Great Lakes region changed from tundra to forests of cedar and pine along with deciduous trees such as oak, birch, and maple.

The original giant mammals in the area, such as mastodons, became extinct. But the woods teemed with other game such as birds, squirrels, rabbits, deer, bears, moose, and on the western edge of the region, bison. The Great Lakes—and the thousands of smaller lakes and rivers in the region—offered an almost unlimited supply of fresh fish for the human inhabitants to eat.

People who lived in the southern regions of the Great Lakes area began to farm beans, squash, corn, and other crops around A.D. 1000. Farther north, where the winters were too long and the soil too poor for agriculture, natives subsisted by hunting, fishing, and gathering nuts and berries. In spite of such a harsh climate, nature's bounty allowed dozens of Native American tribes to grow and prosper.

Although there were dozens of tribes and related clans in the area, the Great Lakes region was populated by two general groups of Native Americans. The Six Nations of the Iroquois (pronounced

Despite the harsh climate of the Great Lakes, Native Americans were able to grow beans, squash, corn, and other crops.

IR-uh-kwoy) lived in the northeastern part of the Great Lakes around the Lake Ontario region of what is now the United States and Canada. The natives of the Algonquian (al-GAHN-kwian) language tribes, known as the Three Fires tribes, lived in the western region around the other Great Lakes.

Tribes of the Northeastern Great Lakes

The Cayuga, Mohawk, Oneida, Onondaga, Seneca, and later the Tuscarora, were six tribes collectively known as the Iroquois Nation, the Iroquois League, or the Six Nations of the Iroquois. These tribes spoke different dialects of the Iroquoian language but were related by custom and tradition. The Iroquois called themselves the Hodenosaunee, meaning "People of the Longhouse."

Members of the Huron tribe, who lived between Lakes Ontario and Huron in present-day Canada, were bitter enemies of the Iroquois and were never members of the Iroquois League, though they were related through language and culture.

The tribes of the Iroquois Nation occupied a wide-ranging territory comprising New York's Mohawk River valley and the Finger Lakes region, bordered on the north by Lake Ontario and the Adirondack

Tribal Names

European and American writers of past centuries had a difficult time understanding all the different tribes and clans that Native Americans divided themselves into. In addition, tribal names can be confusing because alternate names are sometimes used and because different spellings often exist for the same name. Native Americans almost always had different names for their tribes than were given to them by white people. Some names, usually the unflattering ones, were given to tribes by rival tribes. To complicate matters, early historians applied names inconsistently.

French historians, explorers, and traders used French names for tribes while English people used English names. Since Native American languages did not employ writing, tribal names were often crude written translations of Native American pronunciations.

The name *Algonquian* or *Algonquin* or Algonkin is an example of possible confusion. Over time, different writers used altered spellings. To add to the confusion, the word is sometimes used to discuss one small Canadian tribe, the Algonquin, who originally held the name. Other times it is used to describe many different tribes who spoke a common language but who were spread across the northeastern United States, Canada, and elsewhere.

Mountains and on the south by the Catskill Mountains and what today is the New York–Pennsylvania state line. Some tribes also lived in Canada along the northern shore of Lake Ontario.

In 1851 Lewis Henry Morgan wrote a definitive book, *League of the Ho-de-no-sau-nee or Iroquois,* that is still considered a classic in Native American research. According to Morgan,

> Among the Indian nations whose ancient seats were within the limits of our republic, the Iroquois have long continued to occupy the most conspicuous position. They achieved for themselves a more remarkable civil organization, and acquired a higher degree of influence, than any other race of Indian lineage, except those of Mexico and Peru. In the drama of European colonization, they stood, for nearly two centuries, with an unshakable front, against the devastations of war, the blighting influence of foreign intercourse and the still more fatal encroachments of a restless and advancing border population.[3]

The Mohawk were the most feared members of the Iroquois Nation—which is suggested by their name, a word meaning "eaters of men." This name was given to the Mohawk by their enemies because they sometimes practiced cannibalism. Mohawk warriors believed that by eating small pieces of their enemies they would absorb their enemy's strength. But the

Mohawk called themselves "People of the Place of Flint." They were the easternmost tribe of the Iroquois League, and since the league was thought of as a huge longhouse that extended across a large stretch of territory, the Mohawk were "the Keepers of the Eastern Door."

The Cayuga (kay-YOO-guh) traditionally lived in an area near modern-day Syracuse, New York. Their name means the "People at the Landing" or "People at the Mucky Land." They were bordered on the east by the Onondaga (ahn-uhn-DAW-guh), whose name means "People on the Mountain" in their native tongue. The Onondaga homeland was in central New York in an area surrounding the Finger Lakes.

The Finger Lakes

The Finger Lakes are a series of long narrow lakes formed eons ago by glaciers in west central New York State. From west to east, the principal lakes are Conesus, Hemlock, Canadice, Honeoye, Canandaigua, Keuka, Seneca, Cayuga, Owasco, Skaneateles, and Otisco. The lakes vary in length from 11 to 40 miles and are up to 3.7 miles wide.

The Finger Lakes were formed during the last Ice Age, between ten thousand and fourteen thousand years ago. Seneca Lake, which is 67 square miles in area and 617 feet deep, is the largest Finger Lake. These lakes, which lie approximately 30 miles south of Lake Ontario, were home to several tribes of the Six Nations of the Iroquois, including the Seneca, Cayuga, and Onondaga.

From earliest times, the Oneida (oh-NY-duh) tribe inhabited a region of central New York State north of modern-day Binghamton on the southern edge of the Finger Lakes.

The Seneca traditionally lived in a territory between the Genesee River in northwestern New York and Seneca Lake. By the seventeenth century about five thousand Seneca lived in 150 clans grouped into four different settlements.

The Huron tribe lived in what is today south-central Ontario, Canada, on Georgian Bay, an inlet of Lake Huron. The name *Huron* was given to the tribe by the French, and it means something close to "boorish" or "rough." The name they call themselves is Wendat or Wyandot, meaning "islanders" or "peninsula dwellers." Natives of this tribe who lived in what is now Canada were called Huron while those who migrated to territory now in the United States were known as Wyandot.

The Tuscarora (tuhs-kuh-RORH-uh) were an Iroquoian-speaking tribe who lived in numerous villages along the rivers of present-day North Carolina during the seventeenth century. After losing a war with English settlers in Virginia, South Carolina, and North Carolina, the Tuscarora were invited north to join the Iroquois League. They settled in northern Pennsylvania and New York and

writings by missionaries and explorers. The Iroquois were great statesmen, and their tribes were organized into the Iroquois League as early as 1570.

Two men were responsible for bringing the tribes together. Deganawida the Peace Maker was a Huron prophet who had a vision of the tribes united under the sheltering branches of a "Tree of Great Peace" after his tribe was practically wiped out by musket-wielding Iroquois in 1651. The book *500 Nations* by Alvin M. Josephy Jr. describes how the league was born:

One year, a visionary Huron elder named Deganawida appeared in the Iroquois territory, preaching a powerful message of peace. In his travels, he met an Onondaga man named Hiawatha, who was himself caught in the violence of the time. Hiawatha listened to the message of Deganawida. The Peace Maker, as Deganawida was becoming known, conceived of thirteen laws by which people and nations could live in peace and unity—a democracy where the needs of all would be accommodated without violence and bloodshed. To a modern American, it would suggest a society functioning under values and laws similar to those of the Ten Commandments and the U.S. Constitution

Occupying a large territory, the Iroquois had a high degree of influence on other Native American tribes.

in 1722 became the sixth nation of the Iroquois. In 1797 the newly formed U.S. government granted the Tuscarora a reservation near Niagara Falls in New York.

The Workings of the Iroquois League

Much is known about the Iroquois tribes from archaeological studies and historical combined. Each of its laws included a moral structure. [Deganawida said:] "In all of your . . . acts, self-interest shall be cast away. . . . Look and listen for the welfare of the whole people, and have always in view not only the present, but also the coming generations . . . the unborn of the future Nation."

Hiawatha became a supporter of the Peace Maker and his Great Law and, because of his strong oratorical skills, was its principal spokesman, constructing, according to legend, the first wampum belt, a beaded system of coded information employed in reciting the Great Law. Then, with this system for recording and expressing their beliefs, both Deganawida the Peace Maker and Hiawatha took the word to each of the most powerful leaders among the five tribes.[4]

The Iroquois League was modeled after the Native American family, clan, and community organizations that were already in place. The purpose of the league was to unite its members through symbolic kinship while still maintaining the independence of individual tribal members.

Leaders of the league were selected by each tribe's women. According to *500 Nations,*

Hiawatha brought together several tribes under the Great Law using the wampum belt, a system he designed for recording information.

The women of every clan selected the most respected woman among them to be the clan mother. The clan mothers, in turn, appointed the male chiefs to represent the clans at the Grand Council. In this way, the men most trusted by their people for wisdom, integrity, vision, fairness, oratorical ability, and other statesmanlike qualities were given the responsibility of the Great Law.[5]

The Grand Council was made up of fifty life-appointed male sachems, or peace chiefs. The Onondaga had fourteen sachems, the Cayuga ten, the Oneida and Mohawk nine each, and the Seneca eight. Council members were responsible for keeping peace, representing the body of tribes to outsiders, and coordinating group actions in warfare against outsiders.

Major decisions by the league's leadership required a unanimous vote. Likewise, any individual sachem who did not tend to his duties could be impeached through proceedings initiated by his tribe's headwoman. Because it was centrally located, the homeland of the Onondaga tribe was chosen as the meeting place for the annual Grand Council of the Iroquois League.

The Onondaga were the designated "keepers of the fire" and "wampum keepers," and their homeland thus became the unofficial capital and the storage site for the national archives of the league.

It was a great honor to become a sachem, but men who took the position were expected to forfeit any material gain from their position. This point was made by Cadwallader Colden in *The History of the Five Nations of Canada,* written in 1727:

Wampum

Tiny seashell beads fashioned into belts and other articles were called wampum. To the Iroquois and other tribes, these items had great spiritual value. Legend had it that wampum led to the founding of the Iroquois League when Hiawatha, mourning the death of his wife and daughters, met with Deganawida, who consoled the grieving man with a string of white shells; hence the name *wampum,* which in Algonquian means "strings of white."

The Iroquois had a rich oral tradition but lacked a written language. Wampum were used as memory aids to record tribal history and sacred pacts between tribes. This was done through bead color and design. White beads meant purity, and white beads reddened with ocher meant war. Purple beads stood for grief. A row of beads in the shape of diamonds meant friendship while a row of beads in squares signified the council fire. The information conveyed by the wampum's design and colors was memorized by tribal wampum keepers or historians and passed from generation to generation.

To create a wampum string, an artist hammered off portions of seashells, then clamped each fragment in a wooden vise. The shell piece was then shaped into a bead with a grindstone. Next, a hole was drilled in the bead with the aid of a bow drill in which the string of a small bow was pulled rapidly back and forth on a sharp stone drill. Finally, the beads were strung together using a wooden loom.

Although wampum had a spiritual, rather than a monetary, value to Native Americans, when European fur traders saw how much the Iroquois valued wampum, the white men began to use it as a form of money in trades.

[The great Iroquois] Men, both Sachems and Captains, are generally poorer than the common People; for they affect to give away and distribute all the Presents or Plunder they get in their Treaties or in War, so as to leave nothing to themselves. There is not a Man in the Ministry of the Five Nations, who has gain'd his Office, otherwise than by Merit; there is not the least Salary, or any Sort of Profit, annexed to any Office, to tempt the Covetous or Sordid; but, on the contrary, every unworthy Action is unavoidably attended with the Forfeiture of their Commission; for their Authority is only the Esteem of the People, and ceases the Moment that Esteem is lost.[6]

The Iroquois League collapsed in the late eighteenth century when war and diseases brought in by white people decimated the tribes. Before its collapse, the Iroquois League dominated territory as far west as the Mississippi River.

The Rules of the Iroquois League

The Six Nations of the Iroquois were governed by the Iroquois League, whose authority was much like the modern Congress of the United States. The league met once a year to solve problems and make rules. *500 Nations* by Alvin M. Josephy Jr. excerpts the opening invocation of the league.

"Whenever the statesmen of the League shall assemble for the purpose of holding a council, the Onondaga statesmen shall open it by expressing their gratitude to their cousin statesmen, and greeting them, and they shall make an address and offer thanks to the earth where men dwell, to the streams of water, the pools and the lakes, to the maize and the fruits, to the medicinal herbs and trees, to the forest trees for their usefulness, and to the animals that serve as food and give their pelts for clothing, to the great winds and the lesser winds, to the Thunderers; to the Sun, the mighty warrior; to the moon, to the messengers of the Creator who reveal his wishes, and to the Great Creator who dwells in the heavens above who gives all the things useful to men, and who is the source and the ruler of health and life.

Then shall the Onondaga statesmen declare the Council open. . . . All the business . . . shall be conducted by the two combined bodies of Confederate statesmen. First the question shall be passed upon by the Mohawk and Seneca statesmen, then it shall be discussed and passed by the Oneida and Cayuga statesmen. Their decision shall then be referred to the Onondaga statesmen, the Firekeepers, for final judgment."

Some historians have suggested that the democratic political organization of the Iroquois League was closely studied by Benjamin Franklin, George Washington, and the other framers of the U.S. Constitution. This has led to the speculation that the Constitution and the U.S. government structure were partially based on the Iroquois League. But according to author Alvin M. Josephy Jr., "The new United States did not go as far as the Hodenosaunees [Iroquois], for, unlike the Indians, it did not accord equality to all men and both genders among its people."[7]

Tribes of the Western Great Lakes Region

Although the Iroquois League dominated the eastern Great Lakes region, the land farther to the west was populated by the tribes of the Upper Great Lakes. Most of these tribes were speakers of the Algonquian language.

According to George Irving Quimby in his 1960 book *Indian Life in the Upper Great Lakes,*

> The Indian tribes of the Upper Great Lakes region . . . were the Huron, Ottawa, Chippewa [also called] Ojibwa, Potawatomi, Winnebago, Menomini [or Menominee], Sauk, Fox, and Miami. These at least are the tribes that

Some historians believe that the framers of the U.S. Constitution were in part inspired by the democratic organization of the Iroquois League.

would have been counted by the first census taker, had there been one in the region at the time.

There were no census takers, but from the reports and diaries of European explorers, missionaries, and fur traders estimates of population have been obtained, and these provide the basis for the first census of the Upper Great Lakes region.

The Algonquians: A Widely Distributed People

The Algonquian tribes lived in the northeast woodlands and shared a common culture. The Algonquians are divided into more specific groups, including the New England Algonquians (the Massachuset, Mohegan, and Pequot tribes), the Great Lakes Algonquians (such as the Ottawa, Potawatomi, and Ojibwa), and the Prairie Algonquians (such as the Sauk and the Fox). Other Algonquians migrated far to the west, including the Arapaho, Blackfoot, and Cheyenne tribes.

It is often the northeastern and Great Lakes Algonquians that historians are referring to when they use the name *Algonquian* because these tribes played important roles in both American and Canadian history. Since so many Native Americans of Algonquian ancestry lived in these areas, they were the first natives to have contact with the Pilgrims, the French fur traders, and other early European explorers.

Tribes classified as Algonquians spoke the Algonquian language, which is made up of many different dialects, or regional variations. Much as French, Italian, and Spanish have the same roots, many Native Americans spoke different Algonquian dialects that were as distinct from one another as those European languages are. All of the dialects had some vocabulary, grammar, and pronunciation in common, but they also had many differences. Many words in modern English come from the Algonquian language, including hickory, moccasin, moose, papoose, powwow, squash, tomahawk, wigwam, and woodchuck.

There were . . . 3,000 to 3,500 Ottawa Indians; some 25,000 to 35,000 Indians among the various bands of the Chippewa tribe; 4,000 Potawatomi Indians; 3,800 persons in the Winnebago tribe; 3,000 Menomini Indians; 3,500 [Sauk] Indians; 3,000 Fox Indians, and 4,500 persons in the Miami tribe.

These estimates suggest that there was a population of at least 100,000 Indians occupying the Upper Great Lakes. . . . About 10 percent of the [North American Indians] seemed to have lived in the Upper Great Lakes region.[8]

According to Native American legend, the tribes of the western Great Lakes region originated from the Anishinabe people who migrated from the Atlantic region. Along the way, the Anishinabe kept their campfires burning with fire brought from their original homeland. The Anishinabe eventually split into three groups, the Potawatomi, the Ottawa, and the Ojibwa (sometimes spelled Ojibway). The tribes that descended from these groups acknowledged their common past by referring to their collective tribes as "the Three Fires." Each group assumed a different role in sustaining their culture.

The Potawatomi (paht-uh-WHAT-uh-mee) were assigned the task of guarding the sacred fire that was brought from the East. The Ottawa were given the task of maintaining trade with other tribes. The Ojibwa (oh-JIB-wah) (or Chippewa) were to protect and nurture the tribe's deeply held spiritual beliefs. From the ranks of the Ojibwa would emerge the Midewiwin, who would preserve the sacred philosophies of their people in stories, songs, and symbols carved into birch bark.

The Ottawa found homes on islands at the northern end of Lake Huron and the nearby mainland in what is today the Canadian province of Ontario. Members of the Ottawa tribe became such energetic traders that they would walk several hundreds of miles to exchange goods with other tribes.

The Potawatomi settled in the southern part of present-day Michigan, between Lakes Huron and Michigan. Fish and game were abundant there, and the soil and climate were beneficial for farming. The Potawatomi farmed in the summer, went north to hunt game in the fall, and traveled to the prairies to hunt buffalo in the spring. As keepers of the sacred fire, the Potawatomi were known for their diplomatic qualities and their hospitality to visitors. In their role as peace makers, they brought rival tribes together for feasts and to arbitrate disputes.

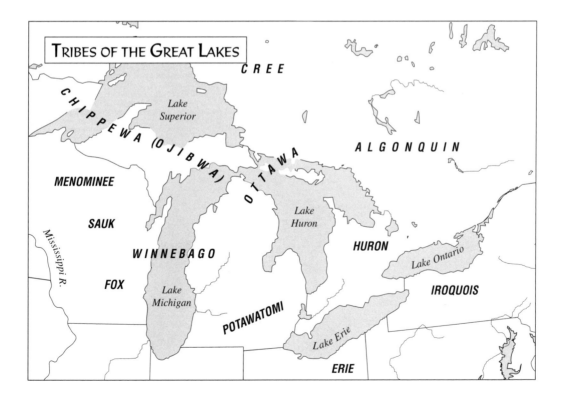

TRIBES OF THE GREAT LAKES

CREE

CHIPPEWA (OJIBWA)

Lake Superior

OTTAWA

ALGONQUIN

MENOMINEE

Lake Huron

SAUK

HURON

Mississippi R.

WINNEBAGO

Lake Ontario

FOX

Lake Michigan

IROQUOIS

POTAWATOMI

Lake Erie

ERIE

The Ojibwa, as guardians of the spiritual traditions of the Anishinabe, continued to be guided by sacred signs. These signs led them far to the north, along the shores of Lake Superior. There they lived on the whitefish that at times choked the rapids of modern-day St. Marys River between Lakes Superior and Huron. Others continued to fan out around Lake Superior to the west, in the modern-day states of Wisconsin and Minnesota and the western part of what is now the Canadian province of Ontario. According to legend, the band of Ojibwa that migrated to the western edge of Lake Superior was blessed with a vision to found the village of La Pointe on Madeline Island, which later emerged as the spiritual center of Ojibwa culture.

Tribes Linked to the Three Fires

The tribes of the Three Fires were linked to other tribes in the Great Lakes region who shared similar customs and who also spoke Algonquian dialects. The tribes who lived in present-day Wisconsin were the Kickapoo, Sauk, and Fox.

The name *Kickapoo,* in its original form before whites adapted it to English, was Kiwegapw, meaning "he moves about, standing now here, now there." This name originated because the Kickapoo have lived in many different places. The Kickapoo were closely related to the Sauk and the Fox. They originally lived on the eastern shores of Lake Michigan in the modern-day state of Michigan. In the

Some tribes traveled great distances in order to hunt buffalo.

The Legend of the Anishinabe

Several tribes in the Great Lakes region have preserved stories about their people's creation. Printed in *The People of the Lakes* is the creation story of the Anishinabe, or "Original People."

"Before the beginning of the world, only Kitche Manido, the Great Spirit existed. As the all-powerful Creator, Kitche Manido first made the four basic elements—rock, fire, wind, and water. From these he fashioned the sun and stars, Earth and everything on it. He made the trees and plants and all forms of animal life. . . . Last of all he made the two leggeds, the humans. . . .

From Kitche Manido, every part of Creation received a spirit and a purpose in a Circle of Life. The plants would provide food and medicines; the trees would give shelter. The animals would sacrifice their lives to provide food and clothing for humans—the Anishinabe. . . .

The Anishinabe first lived by the Great Salt Sea (the Atlantic Ocean) in the east, but long ago they followed the vision of a megis (cowry shell) that led them westward to the Great Lakes."

For many years the Anishinabe journeyed westward by canoe. They paddled up the St. Lawrence River and past Niagara Falls. During their journey, which lasted many generations, they encountered other tribes and subdued them. Legend has it that the Anishinabe eventually split into three groups—the Potawatomi, the Ottawa, and the Ojibwa.

eighteenth century, after defeating the Illinois tribe, the Kickapoo moved southwest, to what is today the state of Illinois. As white settlers moved into Kickapoo territory in later years and displaced them, the Kickapoo began a long odyssey that took them to Missouri, Kansas, Texas, Mexico, and eventually onto a reservation in Oklahoma.

The Fox are sometimes called the Mesquakie, meaning "Red Earth People." This name is appropriate because in the summer the Fox farmed the reddish soil of eastern Wisconsin. (In the winter, they hunted buffalo on the grasslands near the Mississippi River.) The fox was the symbol of one particular clan in the tribe, but the name was mistakenly given to the entire tribe by white people.

The Sauk, or Sac, tribe's name is derived from the Algonquian word meaning "Yellow Earth People." For much of their history, the Sauk were aligned with the Red Earth People, or the Fox. The Sauk lived north of the Fox along the western edge of Lake Michigan in Wisconsin. Like the Fox, the Sauk farmed in the summer and hunted buffalo in late winter. (In the nineteenth century, the Sauk and Fox tribes would merge and become known as the Sauk and Fox tribe.)

The Miami were part of the Woodlands Algonquian group. They lived in the area south of Lake Michigan, in the forested valleys in what is now Indiana and western Ohio. There are several places called Miami in the United States, but the names have different origins. In the Midwest the name comes from the Miami tribe and means "People of the Peninsula." In Florida the name comes from the name of a Creek Indian village and is unrelated to the Miami tribe.

The Illinois tribe also lived south of Lake Michigan. The word *Illinois* is a French adaptation of the tribe's word meaning "people." The Illinois are members of the Prairie Algonquian group for whom the state of Illinois and the Illinois River are named.

Non-Algonquian Speakers

Another tribe lived in the Great Lakes region but did not speak Algonquian dialects. Members of the Winnebago tribe were speakers of the Siouan language that was used among the Sioux (also called Lakota), Iowa, Oto, and Missouri tribes. The Winnebago lived in eastern Wisconsin, but the tribe's name is actually Algonquian since it was given to the tribe by the Sauk and the Fox. *Winnebago* actually means "People of the Filthy Water" because the tribe lived near modern-day Green Bay, Wisconsin, which was extremely green from the lush growth of algae in the water. The Winnebago's noble name for themselves is Hotcangara, meaning "People of the Big Speech," but the name *Winnebago* has stayed with the tribe throughout the centuries.

<u>**Chapter 2**</u>

Lodges of the Great Lakes Clans

The daily lives of Native Americans in the Great Lakes region were based on the bounty of their natural surroundings. Native Americans ate, worked, slept, and played following the rhythms of the seasons. The rich forests of North America provided food, clothing, shelter, and everything else families needed to survive and thrive. Trees themselves were of extreme importance to the Native Americans of the Great Lakes, as discussed in *America's Fascinating Indian Heritage:*

> Broad-leaved trees thrust their roots deep into the rich soil of valleys and grew so tall and thick that the noonday sun barely filtered through their interlocking branches. A man walking through the glades during the leafy season moved in a weird green glow, his moccasins cushioned by the soft earth. Higher up, on hillsides and mountain slopes, coniferous trees crowded even more closely together—millions of dark, spiky cones, all determined to be vertical. . . .

Except for the lakes and rivers, the primeval forests of northeastern America extended in one vast sweep from the swampy south to the snowy north, from the cliffs and sandbars of the east to the edges of the prairie in the west. In aboriginal times this leafy universe was the home of . . . men, women and children to whom the tree gave protection and sustenance. . . .

> The tree's bark, when peeled, dried, and flattened, became the walls of a house. The same bark, when scraped smooth, curved, and stitched, became a container, a tray, or a canoe. Lopped of its branches and divided by fire into suitable lengths, the tree became a wall of stakes to fortify villages. . . . Fashioned into an 18-inch board, fitted with supporting straps, and suspended from a convenient hook, the tree became a baby frame—a kind of cradle—a safe, comfortable place to hold an infant while the mother was at her chores.[9]

27

The villages were . . . stockaded. Having run a trench several feet deep, around five or ten acres of land, and thrown up the ground upon the inside, they set a continuous row of stakes or palisades in this bank of earth, fixing them at such an angle that they inclined over the trench. Sometimes a village was surrounded by a double or even triple row of palisades.[10]

Although palisades were used in the early centuries, by the seventeenth century the democratic power of the Six Nations prevented war between tribes, and palisades were no longer necessary.

Tree bark was used to make the walls of longhouses as well as canoes.

The Longhouses of the Iroquois

By the seventeenth century, the area that would later become New York State was dotted with longhouse villages of the Iroquois tribes. A typical longhouse village was located on a rise between the fork of two streams, which often provided drinking water for the villagers.

According to Lewis Henry Morgan in *League of the Ho-de-no-sau-nee or Iroquois,* village dwellers needed protection from marauding enemy tribes:

Everyone inside the village lived in longhouses made from elm-wood poles and seasoned sheets of elm bark. Longhouses were rectangular, approximately 18 to 25 feet wide and 50 to 150 feet in length. The length varied according to how many fire pits were inside—each family had a fire pit, and each pit added 20 to 25 feet in length to the building. The roof of the longhouse was arched and stood about 25 feet high at its center.

Painted above the door of each longhouse was the symbol of the clan who lived there. Clans in the Seneca tribe, for example, were named the Bear, the Wolf, the Beaver, the Turtle, the Deer, the Snipe, the Heron, or the Hawk.

Joseph François Lafitau, a Jesuit missionary, had this to say about Iroquois longhouses in the early eighteenth century:

It is not without reason that the name of Hotinnonsioni or Builders of Cabins has been given to the Iroquois; they are indeed the most comfortably lodged of all America. Nonetheless it is not so exclusively their property that it cannot be also applied to the Hurons and to some of their other neighbors, who have adopted the same manner of building.[11]

Longhouse villages were not neat and orderly, as European visitors, accustomed to their cities, might expect. As Morgan writes, the houses were "planted like trees of the forest, at irregular intervals, and over a large area. No attempt was made at a street, or at an arrangement of their houses in a row; two houses seldom fronting the same line. They were merely grouped together sufficiently near for a neighborhood."[12]

A system of trails through the forest connected the tribal villages and also connected the tribe's villages to those of the

Construction of Longhouses

Members of the Six Nations of the Iroquois lived together in large buildings called longhouses. In the eighteenth century, French Jesuit missionary Joseph François Lafitau (1681–1746) recorded the process the Iroquois used to build longhouses. He was quoted in Charles Johnson's *The Valley of the Six Nations.*

"Each of these cabins rests on four posts for each fire which are the base and support of the entire structure. Around the entire circumference [of the longhouse] pickets are planted to secure the pieces of elm bark which form the walls and which are bound together with strips made from the interior coating or inner bark of white wood. The square frame being raised, the roof framing is made with poles bent to

the form of a bow, which also are covered with pieces of bark a fathom [six feet] long and a foot or fifteen inches wide. These pieces of bark lap one over the other like slate. They are secured outside with fresh poles similar to those which form the roof frame underneath, and are still further strengthened by long pieces of saplings split in two. These run along the whole length of the cabin, from end to end, and are fastened to the extremities of the roof, on the sides, or on the wings, by pieces of wood cut with hooked ends, which are regularly spaced for this purpose.

After the body of the building is finished, those for whom it is especially intended work leisurely to embellish the interior and to make the necessary compartments after their usages and needs."

entire Iroquois Nation. Until Europeans brought horses to the region in the seventeenth century, people traveled the trails by foot carrying packs on their backs.

Iroquois tribes were sedentary, meaning that they did not move as a group depending on the season, as nomadic tribes did. After twenty years or so, however, firewood would become scarce, and the soil around longhouse villages would no longer contain enough nutrients to grow crops. The poles and the bark of the longhouses would also begin rotting, and bug infestations would take their toll. At that time, the villages would be moved elsewhere along the riverbanks or to a nearby hilltop.

Inside the Longhouse

Inside the windowless longhouses a number of small fires, spaced about 20 feet apart, would burn along a central corridor. According to Lafitau,

The middle space is always the place of the fire, from which the smoke escapes by an opening made directly above it in the roof, and which serves also to give light. These buildings being without windows are only lighted from above. . . . This opening is closed by one or two movable pieces of bark, which are moved back and forth as desired during the heavy rains or certain winds which

A sedentary tribe, the Iroquois set up longhouses that formed a small village.

would cause a back draft for the smoke, and render the cabins very uncomfortable.[13]

On each side of the longhouse, platforms served as beds and resting places for the families who lived within. The platforms were about six feet high and six feet wide, and they extended the length of the building. These platforms were shut in on all sides except the one facing the fire, and according to Morgan, "Upon these they spread their mats of skins, and also their blankets, using them as seats by day and couches at night."[14] Entire families slept together on these bunks, which were made snug with bearskin rugs and blankets.

The bark that covered the platforms on top served as a closet and storage space for food, weapons, snowshoes, baskets, clothes, dishes, and cooking utensils. Between platforms, charred and dried corn and beans were stored in large chests and tall barrels made of bark. On cross poles near the roof, the winter supply of corn hung in bunches braided together by the husks. Roof supports also held strings of dried apples and squash, hanks of tobacco, and bundles of roots.

The doors of the longhouses were made of pieces of removable bark, suspended outside from the top. Doors were not locked; however, when everyone left the longhouse, the bark doors were secured with bars of wood to keep out marauding village dogs. Those who wanted to protect precious belongings would bury them in holes or hide them in secret places in the longhouse.

Baskets and Utensils

Native American women excelled at the art of basketry. Baskets were made from natural materials such as a plant called flag or from corn husks. Sometimes they were decorated with elaborate designs woven into the basket or painted on with plant dye.

Baskets were made with ingenuity and simplicity and were used in many aspects of daily life. Sieve baskets were woven to perfectly sift finely ground cornmeal. Containers for salt were sometimes woven into forms representing human or animal figures.

Kitchen utensils were often elaborately carved with skill and precision. Ladles and soup spoons might feature totems such as a squirrel, a hawk, or a beaver carved into the handle, or humans might be portrayed in a sitting position or with groups of figures wrestling or embracing. Bowls, pitchers, and other vessels were often made from knots of wood cut from tree trunks. These, too, were decorated with various carvings.

In the winter doors were doubled to protect the inhabitants from the cold. Sometimes the second doors were made from skins or buffalo wool. The longhouses were warm during normal winter weather, but during severe cold spells, which could last seven to ten days, the air

The Appearance of the Iroquois

The Iroquois tribes dressed in clothing made from animal skins or woven from plant fibers. In the summer, however, they wore nothing at all. French explorer Samuel de Champlain was one of the first Europeans to write about the people of the lakes in his book *Voyages of Samuel de Champlain, 1604–1618.* In July 1605, Champlain recorded the appearance of Native Americans (whom he called savages) living along the St. Lawrence River.

"All these savages . . . wear neither robes nor furs, except very rarely: moreover, their robes are made from grasses and hemp, scarcely covering the body, and coming down only to their thighs. They have only the sexual parts concealed with a small piece of leather; so likewise the women, with whom it comes down a little lower behind than the men, all the rest of the body being naked. . . . These people paint the face red, black, and yellow. They have scarcely any beard, and tear it out as fast as it grows. . . . As for weapons, they have only pikes, clubs, bows and arrows."

Iroquois Clans

Tribe members of the Iroquois were divided into clans that served as extended families. Unlike European culture, which traced family descent and inheritance through the male line, Iroquois clans were organized matrilineally, or according to the female line.

The Iroquois used this family lineage system to identify themselves. According to *America's Fascinating Indian Heritage,*

> The longhouse lineage of families was the basic unit of (Iroquois) society. Lineages in turn built up into clans, clans into moieties (that is, half-tribes) and moieties into whole tribes. A young man had to marry outside his clan, preferably with a woman who was not even distantly related to his own mother or her female relatives.[15]

inside the longhouse could be frigid. By necessity, the Iroquois grew used to such temperatures.

In the summer the longhouses were cool inside but were plagued with fleas and bedbugs. The odors of fish drying, tobacco, sweat, and babies also mingled with the heat and the wood smoke to give the large cabins a very noticeable odor.

Such a system helped ensure that children would not suffer from inherited disorders that can result when close relatives marry each other.

Within these clans, the elderly members taught the children, the sick and needy were taken care of, and community responsibilities were carried out. Each man, woman, and child had a well-defined role.

Men hunted, made war, and provided protection for the community. Women gathered wild foods, cooked, made baskets and clothing, and cared for the children. Interaction between the sexes was limited, and people were divided into two classes— male and female. Men spent most of their time with other men, and women spent their time with other women.

Except for men's weapons, all property in the Iroquois village belonged to the women, including farming tools, all clothing, and the longhouses themselves. There were practical reasons why women had so much control over Iroquois politics and possessions: Men were often gone on hunting or war expeditions for weeks at a time. All the work of agriculture, community service, and rearing children was left to the women.

Young boys sharpened their battle skills by playing war games. They were encouraged by their mothers to fight other boys with sham war clubs made from cornstalks. At night boys were told heroic stories of their ancestors' bravery. While young girls helped their mothers with chores or went to work in the fields, boys were free to wander in the woods, often for days at a time, living off berries and small game.

Daily life for early Native Americans consisted of hunting, gathering wild food, cooking, making baskets and clothing, and caring for the children.

Lodges of the Western Great Lakes Tribes

Unlike the sedentary Iroquois, tribes of the western Great Lakes region were mostly nomadic or seminomadic. People in the northern regions, such as the Ojibwa, lived in simple, portable wigwams while tribes in warmer climates kept summer homes similar to Iroquois longhouses. While traveling to winter hunting grounds, however, they adopted the wigwam-style homes of the Ojibwa.

The Sauk, Fox, and Miami originally made their homes in the Lake Michigan region. They were semisedentary—that is, they lived in permanent villages part of the time but traveled at other times. In the summer they were farmers who lived in permanent villages, but in the late winter they were buffalo hunters who lived in temporary wigwams on the prairie. Each spring they would then return to their villages to plant and raise crops.

Iroquois Marriage Customs

The marriage customs of the Iroquois were recorded in 1851 by Lewis Henry Morgan in *League of the Ho-de-no-sau-nee or Iroquois.*

"Marriage was not founded upon the affections . . . but was regulated exclusively as a matter of physical necessity. It was not even a contract between the parties to be married, but . . . between their mothers, acting oftentimes under the suggestions of the matrons and wise-men of the tribes. . . . In a general sense . . . it was under maternal control. . . . In ancient times, the young warrior was always united to a woman several years his senior, on the supposition that he needed a companion experienced in the affairs of life. . . . Thus, it often happened that the young warrior of twenty-five was married to a woman of

forty, and oftentimes a widow; while the widower of sixty was joined to the maiden of twenty. But these were . . . primitive customs; the ages of the parties afterwards drew nearer to an equality. . . .

When a mother considered her son of a suitable age for marriage, she looked about her for a maiden, whom . . . she judged would accord him in disposition and temperament. A negotiation between the mothers ensued, and a conclusion was speedily reached. . . . Not the least singular feature of the transaction, was the entire ignorance in which the parties remained of the pending negotiation; the first intimation they received being the announcement of their marriage, without, perhaps, ever having known or seen each other . . . they received each other as the gift of their parents."

One observer, American army major Morrell Marston, described a typical Sauk village in November 1820:

> The Indians have only one way of building bark huts or summer residences, they are built in the form of an oblong, a bench on each of the long sides about three feet high and four feet wide, parallel to each other, a door at each end, and a passage thro the center of about six feet wide, some of those huts, are fifty to sixty feet long and capable of lodging fifty or sixty persons. Their winter lodges are made by driving long poles in the ground in two rows of nearly equal distances from each other, bending the tops so as to overlap each other, then covering them with mats made of what they call puc-way (roof mat grass) a kind of rushes or flags, a Bearskin generally serves as a door, which is suspended on top and hangs down, when finished it is not unlike an oven with the fire in the center and the smoke omits thro the top.[16]

Unlike the Sauk, Fox, and Miami, the Ojibwa tribes of the western Great Lakes region were nomadic people who continually moved with the seasons. Driven by the harsh winter climate of the upper peninsula of Michigan, the Ojibwa followed a yearly cycle of fishing, hunting, gathering nuts, collecting maple syrup and medicinal herbs, growing corn, and harvesting rice. When each food came into season, the Ojibwa moved to the site best suited for gathering that food.

At each new location, the Ojibwa family built a wigwam. The wigwam could be constructed in less than one day with materials found in abundance in the woodlands. To build a wigwam, Ojibwa men placed wood saplings in the ground in an oval shape about fourteen by twenty feet. The saplings were pulled together in arches while women tied the framework together with ropelike wood fibers. The family then placed birch bark over the structure and covered the doorway with an animal hide. In the center of the wigwam, an open fireplace warmed the inhabitants. When it was time to move, the Ojibwa family would roll up the birch bark covering and take it to the next campsite. The wooden frame was left behind for possible use the next year.

The Ottawa and Potawatomi were culturally similar tribes who also lived in wigwams. The Ottawa lived in northeast Michigan and the Potawatomi lived in western Michigan. Both tribes were semi-sedentary. Ottawa and Potawatomi villages were mainly occupied in the summertime. Their dwellings were dome-shaped wigwams made of saplings covered with mats woven from bulrushes and cattails. Some villages were protected by circular palisades similar to those of the Iroquois. Wigwams were also used at the winter hunting grounds.

Ottawa and Potawatomi wigwams contained all of a family's possessions. According to George Irving Quimby,

> Household furnishings and utensils included woven mats, which when

The Ottawa and Potawatomi lived in villages consisting of dome-shaped wigwams.

spread on the floor served as chairs and when spread on wooden platforms served as beds; big wooden mortars and pestles for pounding corn into meal; woven bags; baskets; boxes or trunks of rawhide; wooden bowls and ladles; and pottery jars.[17]

The Menominee, who inhabited what is today northwestern Wisconsin, lived in wigwams during the winter season. They insulated their shelters on the inside with mats made from cattail reeds. These mats were often beautifully colored with dyes made from blueberries, blackberries, chokecherries, wild plums, bloodroot, and sumac bark. In the summer the Menominee lived outdoors. When it rained, they built open shelters from logs and covered them with bark roofs.

The Dress of the Algonquian Tribes

The people of the lakes were skilled at making clothing and beading and at painting their bodies. According to Quimby,

Both men and women wore clothing made of the skins of deer, bear, and beaver. Both sexes wore moccasins, leggings, and robes. The men wore breech-clouts and shirts with detached sleeves. The women wore skirts reaching their knees and shirts in the winter, but nothing above the waist in the summer. Clothing was decorated with painted bands of red and brown.

Women wore their hair well-combed, oiled, and arranged in a single tress hanging down the back and tied with eelskins. Men wore their hair in a variety of ways. Some shaved half of the head, many left the hair long and hanging, others left a strip of hair running along the midline of the head.

Most of the men painted their faces and bodies with a variety of designs, mostly black and red but also green and violet. The pigment obtained from mineral and vegetal sources was mixed with sunflower oil and bear fat. Some men, particularly among the Tobacco Huron, tattooed their bodies with representations of animals.

Women were not painted or tattooed, but wore necklaces and chains of shell beads around their necks and waists and hanging down in front of their robes and shirts.[18]

Clans of the Western Lakes

The Algonquian-speaking tribes such as the Menominee, Ottawa, Potawatomi, Ojibwa, and Fox were much alike in the way they determined their lineage. Like the Iroquois, each tribe was divided into two groups or moieties. Among the Winnebago, Menominee, and Miami, clans in one moiety were named after birds, the clans in the other after land and water animals.

Each clan was identified by an animal symbol known as a totem. Totems for the Winnebago sky moieties included the Eagle, the Pigeon, and the Thunderbird. The earth moieties were divided into the Bear,

the Wolf, the Snake, the Water-Spirit, the Deer, the Fish, and other totems. The twenty-one distinct Ojibwa totems were also classified by whether they dwelled in the sky, on land, or in the water. The totems included such animals as the Wild Cat, the Pickerel, and the Caribou. Bird clans were named the Goose, the Loon, the Black Duck, and the Kingfisher, among others.

Villages of semisedentary tribes were laid out according to clan lines, with the earth totems living in one area and the sky totems living in another. Every clan had its own lodge, and each clan had its own specialty. The Thunderbirds, for instance, were recognized as referees in arguments and the Bears as warriors who policed the village.

A person looked to his or her totem for guidance in how life should be lived. An Ojibwa named L'Anse explains:

I took [my totem] from my father; he took it from his father, and so on, three or four generations back. My [totem] is the deer. The deer is smart and quick. When a deer wants to

An animal symbol, known as a totem, was used to identify each clan.

drink, he goes up the river a little way from where he crossed, because he won't drink the water that has washed his traces. The deer is my companion; I follow his life. I never need a compass to go through the woods, for I am able to find my way just like a deer.[19]

Marriage among the Great Lakes tribes was governed by moiety, clan, and family relationships. Unlike the matrilineal sys-

Skilled Artisans

Native American women were not only responsible for making clothes but also for decorating them so that their beauty would please the cosmic spirits. Women practiced decorative arts such as quillwork, moose-hair embroidery, and weaving.

Porcupine quills were dyed with plant pigment and appliquéd in ornamental designs onto leather garments, bags, and moccasins. Moose-hair embroidery was practiced by Huron women, who artfully applied dyed hair to birch bark, deerskin, or cloth. Weaving involved nettle fibers and the stringy insides of tree bark, which were braided into sashes and bags. When white traders introduced wool yarn in the 1800s, Indian weavers incorporated it into their art along with two other imports: glass beads and silk ribbons.

tem of the Iroquois tribes, descent among western tribes was traced patrilineally, or along male lines. But as with the Iroquois tribes, marriage never took place between persons of the same totem or family.

Men were considered to be of marriageable age at about twenty, when they were good enough hunters to provide food for a family. Women were of marriageable age at about fifteen, when they were able to do the work of grown women, including building wigwams, gathering wood, tanning hides, and preparing and cooking food. Young women who were not married remained in the care of their mothers and were watched over to ensure that they remained virgins until marriage.

A young woman's virginity was taken very seriously:

An old Red Lake woman . . . [said], "In the old days a boy and a girl never walked together. If a man liked a girl he went to see her in the presence of her parents and then only in daytime, never at night. You never saw a man and a girl alone by themselves. It was awful to see a boy and a girl walk together."[20]

Members of the Ojibwa and other Great Lakes tribes practiced the tradition of arranged marriages. Many times a young woman would not know who she was going to marry until her parents told her on the day of her wedding. Other times, if a young woman strongly objected to her parents' choice of mates, her wishes would be taken into consideration and she did not have to marry the man her parents had chosen for her.

In *Chippewa Child Life,* an Ojibwa medicine man tells of his search for a new wife after his first wife died:

> My first wife died. She was a good woman; I admired her. I went to her uncle (her parents were dead) and asked for her sister. I gave many things to her uncle; quilts that I had received at dances, as well as food. The girl's brother asked her nicely to marry me, and so she did. There was no marriage ceremony.[21]

Eating together and sharing a fur robe used in bedding signified that a couple was married, and no formal ceremony existed.

Polygamy Among Native Americans

Polygamy, or the custom of a man having more than one wife at one time, was practiced among many Native American tribes. Morrell Marston described this custom in 1820:

> Many of these Indians have two wives, the greatest number that I have known any man to have at one time was five. When an Indian wants more than one wife, he generally prefers that they should be sisters, as they are more likely to agree and live together peaceable. An old man of fifty or sixty [who already has two or three wives] will frequently marry a girl of sixteen. . . . It seldom happens that a man separates from his wife, it sometimes does however happen, and then she is at liberty to marry again.[22]

Whether practiced in villages of Ojibwa wigwams or Seneca longhouses, the marriage customs and clan systems of the Great Lakes Native Americans embodied important traditions for the continuing survival of the tribes.

Chapter 3

The Bounty of the Four Seasons

The Great Lakes region covers more than 375,000 square miles. In past centuries, that 750-by-500-mile area featured an incredible abundance of plants and animals that provided a rich diversity of foodstuffs and the raw materials for clothing and shelter for the local Native Americans. Before the arrival of the Europeans in the seventeenth century, Native Americans hunted, fished, and farmed using tools made from stone, wood, and animal parts while staying one step ahead of the changing seasons. After they began trading with the Europeans in the 1600s, Native Americans had axes, rifles, and other iron goods to help them endure.

People of the Lakes describes how the weather affected the lives of the Ojibwa who lived in the frigid region around Lake Superior:

> Winter came early to the people of the lakes. By late September—a time known to the Ojibwa as the Shining Leaf Moon—the birches were turning golden, and the sugar maples were touched with crimson. By October, or the Falling Leaf Moon, chill winds were sweeping down from the northwest, combing the leaves from the branches and raising whitecaps on the blue water. By November, or the Freezing Moon, snow blanketed the forest trails, and woodland creatures were making ready for the long, cold siege that lay ahead. Beavers settled into their lodges, and black bears repaired to their dens.
>
> In their villages, however, it was time for families to count their blessings and move on. The food they had set by during the short growing season— corn and squash from their gardens, berries from the meadows, wild rice from the marshes—would eventually be exhausted in the absence of fresh provisions. To survive the harsh winter, the villagers would have to divide into small groups and set out

for hunting camps, where the men would stalk deer and other game and spear or net fish beneath the ice.

The people planned for this move far in advance, marking the time on calendars of their own devising. "My father kept count of the days on a stick," recalled an Ojibwa woman named Nodinens. . . . "He had a stick long enough to last a year," she added, "and he always began a new stick in the fall. He cut a big notch for the first day of a new moon and a small notch for each of the other days."[23]

To survive in the winter, men would divide into small groups to fish and hunt deer and other wild game.

Sugaring in Spring

Spring comes late to much of the Great Lakes region. As the days get longer, the iced-over lakes and rivers begin to thaw while flowers and other early spring plants begin to emerge from the soil. In late March, when the sap begins to flow in the maple trees, tribes move from their winter hunting grounds to maple-sugaring areas.

Maple sugar was eaten plain, mixed with water, or sprinkled over a variety of foods. It was the primary seasoning used by Great Lakes tribes, who put it on every kind of food, much like people use salt today. Iroquois hunters could spend days hunting in the forest surviving on little more than dried corn flour and maple sugar mixed with water.

To collect the raw sap, entire villages moved deep into the woods. Each family had its own stand of maple trees, which they called sugarbush. To tap the trees, a gash was made in each tree trunk a few feet off the ground. A spout made from cedar wood was hammered into the cut and the sap would trickle into a birch-bark pail beneath the spout. After each tree was drained, the sap was collected and poured into an even larger birch-bark container.

Rocks heated white-hot over a campfire were dropped into the filled container,

bringing the sap to a boil. The heat reduced the liquid first to syrup, then to sugar. When each family had a year's supply of maple sugar, the tribe broke camp and returned to its permanent village. The tribes consumed a portion of the harvest in a ceremonial prayer and feast. Some of the sugar was also sprinkled on the graves of ancestors to "feed" the spirits of the dead.

Fishing

While the women were preparing the maple sugar, the men often ventured from camp to fish in lakes and streams. No one laid claim to any part of a river's bank or to any part of a lake. As anthropologist Mary Inez Hilger explains,

> Indians have a tradition that Lake Superior and the large lakes are theirs for fishing but that inland lakes should be left unmolested. [One Native American man said:] "I often heard my father say the old Indians believed the inland lakes and woods belonged to the animals. They would never bathe in inland lakes."[24]

In order to collect raw sap, Native Americans hammered a spout into the base of a maple tree, letting the sap trickle into a pail beneath it.

In the early spring, a thick layer of ice often still covered the lakes, and the men had to cut through it to reach

Thanks to the Maple

Among the Iroquois tribes, the first festival of spring was the Maple Dance, in which the Native Americans gave thanks to the maple tree for its sweet syrup. This ritual was observed by Lewis Henry Morgan, who wrote about it in 1851 in his book *League of the Ho-de-no-sau-nee or Iroquois.*

"The primary idea of this ceremonial was to return thanks to the maple itself; but at the same time they rendered their thanks to the Great Spirit for the gift of maple. . . .

The opening speech was then delivered, by one of the keepers of the faith. The following, made at the opening of one of the councils among the Senecas, is in the usual form. . . .

'Friends and Relatives. . . . The season when the maple tree yields its sweet waters has again returned. We are all thankful that it is so. We therefore expect all of you to join in our general thanksgiving to the maple. We also expect you to join in a thanksgiving to the Great Spirit, who has wisely made this tree for the good of man. We hope and expect that order and harmony will prevail. . . .'"

When these speeches and exhortations concluded, the dance, which was a prominent feature of their religious festivals, was announced.

---

the fish. After puncturing the ice, a fisherman would lie flat on his stomach with his head and arms over the hole. He then covered his head with a blanket to block out the sunlight and allow him to see into the water's depths. When a fish came into view, the fisherman would quickly spear it and pull it from the water.

The people of the lakes region fished year round for herring, trout, sturgeon, carp, whitefish, pickerel, and other species. But springtime was the season when some species of fish were mating. When the ice melted, sturgeon left the Great Lakes to swim up rivers to spawn. Unlike salmon, which die after spawning, sturgeon remain alive and swim back to the lakes. Native Americans would snare them on their return journey, thereby allowing the fish to breed before dying. The fish that escaped the fishermen would live to spawn the next year's catch.

To catch sturgeon, Native Americans constructed a framework of poles across the river. First, they anchored heavy poles vertically in the river and then lashed on timber crosspieces for people to sit on. Between the poles they strung basswood cord back and forth until it formed a strong netting that would trap the fish. People sitting on the framework then caught the fish with hooks and killed them with clubs.

According to one nineteenth-century writer, the Menominee were observed "spearing the sturgeon in the river. For this purpose they use only small canoes, very light, in which they stand upright; and in the middle of the current spear the sturgeon with an iron-pointed pole." [25]

At other times, tribes used netting to catch fish. Each night, nets attached to stakes were laid in shallow waters. The nets were sprinkled with the powdered roots of certain plants known to attract fish. Sometimes small bells were also attached to the netting to inform the fishermen that a fish had become ensnared in the net.

Once caught, there were many ways to prepare fish. Some might be roasted or boiled in a stew with cornmeal, but much of the catch would be preserved for times when fish were scarce. If the temperatures were cold enough, the fish might be buried in the snow to be frozen. In warm months, the fish were cleaned and their flesh was dried in the sun or over a fire. These dried fillets were then mixed with maple sugar and packed into birch-bark containers for storage.

Bark Canoes

Canoes made from tree bark were used by Native Americans throughout the Great Lakes region. They were utilized for traveling on lakes and rivers in order to fish and hunt as well as to move goods and families. Canoes varied in length from twelve feet—which could carry two adults—to forty feet—which could carry up to thirty people. This excerpt from *Chippewa Child Life* discusses the bark canoes used by the Ojibwa.

"The bark canoe of the Chippewa is, perhaps the most beautiful and light model of all the water crafts ever invented. They are generally made complete with the rind [bark] of one birch tree, and so ingeniously shaped and sewed together, with roots of the tamarack, which they call *wat-tap,* that they are water-tight, and ride upon the water, as light as a cork. They gracefully lean and dodge about, under the skillful balance of an Indian . . . but like everything wild, are timid and treacherous under the guidance of a white man. . . .

Although both men and women made canoes, canoe making was usually considered to be a man's occupation. . . . The men did the work requiring the use of tools, such as shaping the wood for ribs, floor, bow, and stern. The women prepared the bark and the pitch, and did the sewing. All the material used in making the canoe came from trees: the bark was of the birch; the gunwales, ribs, and flooring of green cedar saplings; thread, of the split roots of spruce; and pitch, of spruce resin."

Some tribes used netting sprinkled with powdered roots of plants to attract and catch fish.

Farming in Summer

At the end of the maple sugar and fishing seasons, the final frosts of early May gave way to the summer farming season. Those tribes who planted crops then moved to their summer villages.

Each family had its own garden. Men would till the soil with old axes, bones, or any tool that would break the ground. Some made wooden hoes while others used the shoulder blades from a large deer or moose. Once the soil was turned over, women planted seeds for corn, beans, and squash in rows of small clusters called hillocks. After the seeds were sown, a spiritual leader, or shaman, would appeal to the spirits for a bountiful harvest.

One tribe, the Seneca, grew three varieties of corn. According to Lewis Henry Morgan,

The White (*O-na-ó-ga-ant,*) the Red, (*Tic-ne,*) and the White Flint (*Ha-gó-wä*). . . . The white flint ripens first, and is a favorite corn for hommony; the red next, and is used principally for charring and drying; the white last, and is the corn most esteemed by the Indians. It is used for bread, and supplies the same place with them that wheat does with us.[26]

Much of the food grown in gardens was preserved for use later in the year. Squash was sliced into pieces and smoked or dried in the sun. Corn was dried and stored whole or ground into meal, and any surplus was stored in underground caches lined with birch bark. In 1851 Morgan wrote about the caches of the Iroquois:

The Iroquois were accustomed to bury their surplus corn, and also their charred green corn, in caches, in which the former would preserve uninjured through the year, and the latter for a much longer period. They excavated a pit, made a bark bottom and sides, and having deposited their corn within it, a bark roof, water tight, was constructed over it, and the whole covered up with earth. Pits of charred corn are still found near their ancient settlements. Cured venison and other meats were buried in the same manner, except that the bark repository was lined with deer-skins.[27]

Part of the harvest was steamed, roasted, or boiled and eaten immediately. Members of the Winnebago tribe had a complex process for cooking large amounts of corn. First, they pounded the ears of corn on a rack to separate the kernels from the cob. Next, they put the grain in a pit on top of red-hot stones lined with husks. Finally, they laid another layer of husks on top of the kernels. Water was poured in the pit and dirt was piled on top of everything. The next morning, the delicious, steamed corn was ready to be eaten. Although corn was abundant in late summer, gluttony was frowned upon and children were warned against it. Old folk tales even recounted that "too many corn cakes dripping with maple syrup would bring on the bogeyman Longnose."[28]

Gathering Wild Food

While waiting for the crops to grow, villagers fished, hunted, and gathered wild foods. Women and children (as well as men of the Winnebago tribe) picked a wide variety of wild berries, including gooseberries, raspberries, and blueberries. After everyone ate their fill of the fresh berries, the leftovers were dried or preserved. Blueberries were dried whole on frames constructed of reeds. Raspberries were cooked into a paste and were then spread over sheets of birch bark. The sun would dry the paste into small thin cakes, which were then tied in bundles for storage.

Many other activities took place during the summer season in Native American communities around the Great Lakes. This was a time when many wild plants were at the peak of their growth, and women and children were busy gathering their bounty.

In the realm of the Iroquois, lush forest clearings provided a wide variety of edible plants such as wild greens, skunk cabbage, and pokeweed. Young milkweed shoots less than four inches in height were eaten boiled and flavored with animal fat. Pumpkin blossoms were cooked with meat into a flavorful soup while pumpkin seeds were dried and eaten. A tea made from boiled raspberry twigs, wintergreen, and other herbs was served with meals. Likewise, trees yielded acorns, walnuts, and hickory nuts, which were eaten whole, ground into flour, or pressed into oil.

Other Uses of Wild Plants

Of course, not all plants were used for food. In the western lakes region, the Algonquian-speaking tribes harvested the fibers from the inner bark of the basswood tree. This soft yellow material was cut into strips and woven into baskets or formed into containers for liquid. The finest strands were made into twine for sewing mats and other household items.

The stalks of the wood nettle plant were equally useful when wound together into twine. Finer wood nettle cord was used to weave clothing while coarse twine was used to make animal traps and fishnets. Knotting the twine into nets was a painstaking, time-consuming job. In spite of this, some Ojibwa fishnets were over two hundred feet long. The fiber of the native hemp plant was also used to fashion cords, nets, and baskets.

Believing that the grain of wild rice was sacred and could not be cultivated by humans, the Ojibwa had many taboos about the harvesting of rice.

At the height of the summer, huge quantities of bulrushes and cattails were harvested. The Ojibwa and other western Great Lakes tribes dyed these plants and then wove them on a wooden frame or loom, producing floor mats and wall coverings with patterns such as stripes and diamonds.

Tanning Hides

The people of the lakes generally hunted in the winter when animals were not bearing and nursing their young. Deer, however, were hunted throughout the year. Deer were plentiful and provided venison as well as antlers and bones for tools, sinew and guts for bindings, and hides for clothing.

In the summer, the chore of tanning animal hides fell to women. Tanning was a difficult day-long process. After the hide was removed from the animal, it was soaked to soften it. The damp skin was then thrown over a post set into the ground at an angle, and the women used a bone or stone tool to scrape the hide clean of flesh and hair. The hide was further softened by soaking it in a solution made from the boiled brain of the deer. The hide was then rinsed, laced to a frame, and stretched to

Moccasins

Soft shoes known as moccasins were invented by Native Americans. Lewis Henry Morgan praises the shoe (which he spelled *moccason*) in his book *League of the Ho-de-no-sau-nee or Iroquois.*

"[The moccason] is true to nature in its adjustment to the foot, beautiful in materials and finish, and durable as an article of apparel. It will compare favorably with the best single article for the protection and adornment of the foot ever invented. . . .

The moccason is made of one piece of deerskin. It is seamed up at the heel, and also in front, above the foot, leaving the bottom of the moccason without a seam. In front the deer-skin is gathered, in place of being crimped; over this part porcupine quills or beads are worked, in various patterns. The plain moccason rises several inches above the ankle . . . and is fastened with deer strings; but usually this part is turned down, so as to expose a part of the instep, and is ornamented with bead-work. . . . A small bone near the ankle joint of the deer, has furnished the moccason needle from time immemorial; and the sinews of the animal the tread."

The Wild Rice Harvest of Late Summer

For the tribes in the Lake Superior region, late summer was the time to harvest wild rice, which flourished in the marshy lakes in the central and northern parts of present-day Wisconsin and Minnesota.

In late August people left their summer camps to paddle their canoes to the shallow shores of the rice-laden swamps and lakes. By this time the thick stalks of the rice plant grew five feet above the water line and several feet below. The wild rice plants were topped by heavy barbed spikes that concealed kernels of grain.

The wild rice plant was sacred to the Ojibwa, who believed that the grain could not be cultivated by humans but could only grow wild. This belief underlaid many taboos about harvesting the grain. For example, women who were menstruating could not participate in the harvest, nor could people who had recently lost a family member. Both the Ojibwa and the Menominee believed that monsters lurked under the surface of the lakes and might cause the season's crop to fail if the taboos were broken.

The wild rice harvest was a festive occasion, much like the maple sugar harvest. Families camped together on the shores of

its maximum size. After it dried, this white hide was tinted a light brown hue by smoking it over a fire that was burning damp rotting wood.

After they were dried, deer hides had many uses. They could be made into items such as ceremonial drums or sewn into items of clothing, including breech-clouts, leggings, skirts, dresses, and moccasins.

the lake where the rice grew. Each clan claimed its own spot, which it returned to year after year. As the rice was harvested, some of it was cooked and served alongside freshly caught fish and waterfowl.

Preparing the harvested rice involved several steps. First, the stalks were beaten with sticks to remove the ripe grains. To remove the inedible hulls, the loosened grains were parched over a fire; afterwards they could be cracked free and winnowed out. After the rice harvest was over, Native Americans thanked the spirits.

Extra rice was packed into skin or bark containers and was carried back to the vil-lages. Part of the harvest was stored at the lakeshore camps for use when the tribes returned in the spring. The remainder of the rice was carried on to the winter camps. The ancient tradition of gathering wild rice is still practiced today by many Native Americans who live in Minnesota, Wisconsin, and Canada.

Autumn on the Upper Great Lakes

As autumn arrived, the people of the upper Great Lakes began to prepare for winter. Besides burying their wild rice at their summer camps, they also stored extra

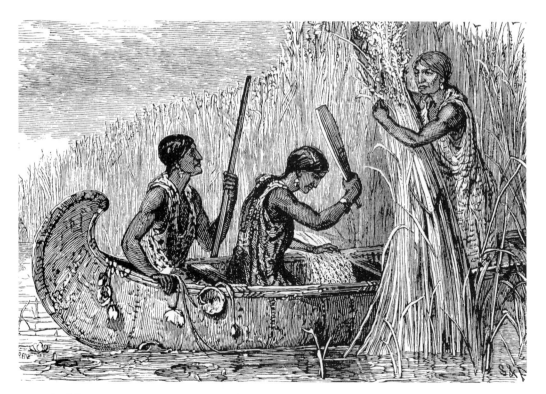

Paddling canoes into shallow waters of rice-laden swamps was one way to collect the natural bounty.

corn, beans, and other dried food. As the days grew shorter and the nights grew colder, gathering a large supply of fish became the main concern of the tribes. In addition, men went into the woods to hunt and trap while women readied for the forthcoming move to the winter hunting camps.

By mid-November snow covered the earth. As the waterways froze over with ice, canoes became useless. The Ojibwa made use of flat-bottomed sleds made from hardwood. These sleds were called *nobugidaban,* or toboggans. Before the arrival of European horses, toboggans were pulled by humans or dogs and were made large enough to carry one or two people and a small load of possessions. Once horses were introduced to the Great Lakes region, tribes in the more moderate southern climates developed large toboggans that could hold entire families along with their gear. In the northern regions, the forests were too thick and the snow too deep for horses to be of much use.

Native Americans who did not ride in toboggans walked through the deep snow using snowshoes, which had frames that were made from hardwood and a netting composed of hide, twine, or sinew. Henry Lee Morgan describes the snowshoes of the Iroquois:

Mosquitoes

The ponds, lakes, and swamps of the upper Great Lakes region were breeding grounds for many species of blood-drinking and biting insects such as the mosquito, black fly, and wood tick. When white traders first traveled to the region and encountered these pests, a few recorded their experiences in their journals. One such writer was Henry Rowe Schoolcraft, who wrote about mosquitoes in his 1821 book *Travels Through the Northwest Regions of the U.S.*

"We passed the . . . night, around our fires . . . prevented from falling asleep by the labour of brushing away the voracious hordes of musquitoes, which unceasingly beset us with their stings, and poured forth their hateful and incessant buzzing in our ears. It cer-

tainly requires a different species of philosophy to withstand, undisturbed, the attacks of this ravenous insect. . . . He who is afflicted, without complaining, by an unexpected change of fortune, or the death of a friend, may be thrown into a fit of restless impatience by the stings of a musquito; and the traveller who is prepared to withstand the savage scalping knife, and the enraged bear, has nothing to oppose to the attacks of the enemy, which is too minute to be dreaded, and too numerous to be destroyed."

Schoolcraft and other travelers to the region would have been less bothered by the ravenous mosquitoes if they smeared bear fat over their exposed skin in the manner of the Ojibwa.

The snow-shoe is an Indian invention. Upon deep snows which accumulate in the forest, it would be nearly impossible to travel without them. . . . The snow-shoe is nearly three feet in length, by about sixteen inches in width. A rim of hickory, bent around with an arching front, and brought to a point at the heel, constitute the frame. . . . Within the area . . . was a woven net-work of deer strings.[29]

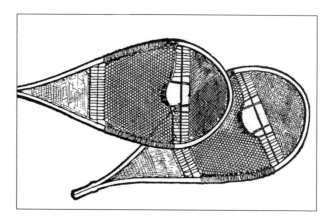

Nearly three feet in length and made from hardwood and sinew or twine, the snowshoe is a Native American invention.

The Winter Camp

Despite the harsh climate, winter was a time to hunt. Animals were easy to track in the deep snow, and they were weakened from hunger. Once skinned, their thick winter coats were extremely useful for keeping people warm.

As in other seasons, Native American men relied on bows and arrows as well as various traps to catch animals. Herbs and other lures were also employed to attract game. Hunting charms were sometimes smoked in a pipe with a bit of tobacco. These charms produced an aroma that might lure an animal out of hiding. At night, a hunter might also use a torch to transfix deer or other game in its light, making them easier to kill.

In early winter, before the waterways froze over, men would hunt beavers, muskrats, ducks, and geese. Some tribes journeyed southwest to the prairies, where buffalo were found in abundance. In mid-

winter, Native American hunters preyed on moose, elks, deer, bears, wolves, foxes, mink, and rabbits. Although hunting was a necessity of survival, Native Americans did not believe in indiscriminate killing of game and thus did not destroy any animal they could not use.

Winter was the time when Native American families in the Great Lakes region lived close together, being confined to their wigwams through the long, cold days and nights. Temperatures could fall to twenty degrees below zero, with winds making the temperature feel like ninety below. Ice on some lakes could be five feet thick, and in a typical winter four to six feet of snow might cover the ground.

Winter wigwams were covered with two layers of overlapping mats to keep out the wind. Before family members went to sleep at night, children played games, women made clothes or beadwork, and men repaired tools and weapons.

Winter evenings in the northern Great Lakes region was also a time for telling stories around the fire while a family member quietly beat a drum. Outside the wolves howled, and the wigwam creaked in the chill wind. People told tales of the spirits who guided the seasons and the plants and animals that clothed and nour-ished them. As stated in *People of the Lakes,* "Families in their shelters knew that all the ingenuity bequeathed to them by their ancestors was not enough to sustain them. It was only through the mercy of the higher powers that they found warmth and safety in the bitter depths of the year."[30]

Chapter 4

Spirits and Healing

From the Iroquois on the southern shores of Lake Ontario to the Ojibwa on the northwestern edge of Lake Superior, the clans of the lakes held strong spiritual beliefs. The clans believed that their natural surroundings were permeated with spirits. These spirits could be either helpful or harmful, depending on how they were treated. Spirits were believed to govern the actions of all plants, animals, rocks, and weather phenomenon. Native Americans spent much of their time praying to these spirits, pondering their motives, and making offerings to appease them.

The people of the lakes believed in the concept of a supreme being, or Great Spirit, who was without form and had little contact with humans. The Great Spirit was an ever-present active force who oversaw the entire Earth. In 1851 Lewis Henry Morgan explained his understanding of the Great Spirit:

> The Iroquois believed in the constant superintending care of the Great Spirit. He ruled and administered the world, and the affairs of the [Indians]. . . . the Iroquois regarded the Great Spirit as the God of the Indian alone. They looked up to him as the author of their being, the source of their temporal blessings, and the future dispenser of the felicities [happiness] of their heavenly home. To him they rendered constant thanks and homage for the change of the seasons, the fruits of the earth, the preservation of their lives, and for their political prosperity. . . . Their knowledge of the Great Spirit was necessarily limited and imperfect. . . . They could not fully conceive of the omnipresence of the Great Spirit, except through the instrumentality of a class of inferior spiritual existences, by whom he was surrounded.[31]

The belief in the Great Spirit was common among all of the tribes in the Great

In this eighteenth-century drawing, the Iroquois give thanks to the Great Spirit.

Lakes region, and the concept of the supreme being also underlaid the idea of duality—the idea that life was a constant struggle between light and dark, good and bad.

The Evil Spirit, or Evil Minded, according to legend, was the Great Spirit's brother. As the Great Spirit created humans and all useful animals and products, the Evil Spirit created monsters, poisonous reptiles, and noxious plants. The Great Spirit delighted in virtue and happiness while the Evil Spirit scattered discord and calamities. The Great Spirit could not control the Evil Spirit; that was left to humans, who must trust the Great

Spirit and be obedient to his commands. This obedience would offer refuge from the evil one.

Supernatural Spirits

Along with the Great Spirit, the people of the lakes knew of lesser spiritual forces who made rivers flow, danced with the rain clouds, blew through the trees, and changed the face of the land in the spring, summer, fall, and winter. These lesser spirits could be sources of both good and evil. One example was the Iroquois spirit Hé-no, who created thunder. According to Morgan, "The thunderbolt [was] at once the voice of admonition, and the instrument of vengeance. [The Iroquois] also intrusted to him the formation of the cloud, and the gift of rain."[32]

The three spirits who sustained Iroquois farm crops were called the Three Sisters—the Spirit of Corn, the Spirit of Beans, and the Spirit of Squash. These plants were believed to be the special gift of Hä-wen-né-yu, the Iroquois name for the Great Spirit. The Three Sisters were believed to have the forms of beautiful females who were fond of each other and were delighted to dwell together. The clothing of the Three Sisters was made from the leaves of their respective plants. During the growing season, the sisters visited the farm fields and dwelt among the plants. The trio was known collectively as De-o-há-ko which means "Our Life" or "Our Supporters." The spirits of the Three Sisters could sometimes be seen or heard as they rustled among the corn or shook the stems of the squash.

Iroquois Harvest Ceremonies

The people of the lakes believed that the spirits helped feed them while hunting, fishing, and farming. Tribes such as the Iroquois Nation, which depended on agriculture, held regular festivals based on the stages of plant growth. The festivals were happy social occasions, but they were also tied to solemn ceremonies in which Native Americans were constantly reminded of the relationship between spirits and humans. These ceremonies featured masked performers who would also seek to cure disease and gather good omens for the tribes.

In the spring, the Maple Festival celebrated the rising of the sap. Later, a Planting Festival was held to seek blessings for the seeds of the vital corn, beans, and squash crops. In early summer, the Wild Strawberry Festival gave thanks to the season's first wild fruits, which were made into jelly in large bark troughs. Late summer saw the four-day celebration of the Green Corn Festival. Each day culminated in a feast that honored the year's first corn crop. The Harvest Festival was a four-day celebration for the autumn gathering of beans and squash. Around this time of year, the Ojibwa in the northwestern Great Lakes region held their Wild Rice Festival to thank the spirits for the sacred grain that insured their survival.

The most important celebration was the New Year Festival, usually held in mid-February. This seven-day festival involved many rituals, including fasting. During this festival people held a belt of white wampum and confessed to any misdeeds and evil thoughts they might have had in the past year. Likewise, people sometimes forced themselves to vomit during the festival, thus cleansing themselves in preparation for a new agricultural year.

Other Native American beliefs dealt with the behavior of the heavens:

> The passage of the seasons and the growth of crops made the people aware of the importance of the calendar. Great respect was paid to the sun, moon and stars; in particular, the Morning Star was very important. . . . The four directions—north, south, east, and west—were important to [Indian] beliefs. In many of the legends, spirits behave in different ways according to which of the four regions their activities took place in. The universe was believed to be directed by spiritual powers of a mysterious nature to whom men must constantly pray for assistance and guidance. Offerings must be made to the first of the harvest, for example, and certain portions of hunted animals.[33]

The Iroquois also believed in a land of the dead. Warrior spirits were believed to live in the sky and were associated with cosmic winter light shows, known today as the aurora borealis, or Northern Lights. There also existed an underworld Mother of Animals who watched over wild game.

Ancestor spirits played a large part in Native American spiritual beliefs. Ancestors watched over the daily activities of tribes and could also be visited at night in dreams. Dream ancestors were to be found living in beautiful villages under the earth, where life was better than on the earth's surface. In these places, the ancestor spirits knew neither war nor disease, and they never lacked skins or food.

The Iroquois Creation Myth

The Iroquois believed in a creation story that told how their people were put on Earth. Since they had no written language, the story was passed down from generation to generation by storytellers.

The Iroquois believed that the first people lived in the sky because there was no Earth. Above the clouds, the chief's daughter became deathly ill. A wise old man told the people to dig up a tree and lay the girl beside the hole. People dug, but as they did, the tree fell through the hole and dragged the chief's daughter with it.

Below was an endless sheet of water where two swans floated. The swans heard a clap of thunder and looked up to see the tree and the girl fall into the water. They saved the girl and took her to the Great Turtle, the master of all animals, who called all the other animals together for a conference.

The animals arrived and the Great Turtle told them that the appearance of the girl was a sign of good fortune for the future. The Great Turtle commanded the animals to find where the tree had sunk so that it could be put on the Great Turtle's back to make an island for the girl to live on.

The swans took the animals to where the tree had fallen. An otter, a muskrat, and a beaver all dived underwater to find the tree but returned to the surface exhausted. Soon they rolled over and died.

The False Face Society

Members of Iroquois clans belonged to many religious organizations. One of the best-known organizations was the False Face Society, whose members wore extravagantly carved masks to cure the sick.

When tribespeople fell ill, False Faces were summoned to their longhouses. Clad in magical masks, the False Faces formed a circle around the sick person. Some danced, shook rattles, and chanted; others scooped up ashes from the fire pit and blew them on the patient. If this medicine magic worked, and the sick person got better, he or she automatically became a member of the False Face Society. It was then necessary for that person to secure a mask. If the person was not up to carving a mask, he or she might ask an artist to do the job.

To make a mask, people found a living basswood tree, burned an offering of tobacco at its base, and then carved the face directly into the living tree. When the mask was near completion, it was cut from the tree, hollowed out, and painted.

Each mask was unique. Some had ornate locks of horse hair, scowling eyes, and tongues sticking out. Others had long pointed noses, crooked mouths with huge lips, and sharp pantherlike teeth.

Masks had to be treated with respect. Owners fed them corn mush and rubbed them with sunflower oil. A person who ridiculed a mask was believed to be destined for illness.

An Iroquois mask and rattle.

Other animals tried and found the same fate. At last old lady toad tried. She was underwater a long time. Finally she surfaced and managed to spit a mouthful of dirt onto the back of the Great Turtle before she died. It was magical earth and grew into a large island where the chief's daughter was placed. The two swans circled it, and soon it grew into the world island that it is today, supported by the waters on the back of the Great Turtle.

Since the island was dark, the Great Turtle decided to light the sky. He sent Little Turtle to climb the dangerous path to the heavens. All the other animals invoked their magic to help Little Turtle find her

Tobacco and the Sacred Pipe

All Native Americans believed that tobacco was a gift from the Great Spirit, and they made frequent offerings of it to gain the goodwill of spirits. When it was nearly time to pick wild rice, for example, a small amount of the dried leaf was tossed on lake waters to insure a good harvest. If someone encountered bad luck, a tobacco offering was also made to ward off evil spirits.

In addition to ritualistic uses, tobacco was used as a social bond between people. Invitations to a ceremony were offered with a pinch of tobacco. Tribes formalized peace treaties with the communal smoking of tobacco and herbs. Important occasions warranted the use of a long ornate pipe called a calumet, which had a feather-decorated pipe stem and an intricately carved stone bowl.

In a report for the U.S. National Museum in 1897, nineteenth-century writer Joseph McGuire elaborated on the custom of tobacco smoking. He was quoted in editor Emma Helen Blair's *The Indian Tribes of the Upper Mississippi Valley and Region of the Great Lakes.*

"No important undertaking was entered upon without deliberation and discussion in a solemn council at which the pipe was smoked with all present. . . . Sometimes the decoration of pipes and their stems has great ceremonial . . . significance."

In *Chippewa Child Life,* Mary Inez Hilger quotes an unnamed Native American who discusses the powers of tobacco.

"My aunt always strews tobacco on the water, all around the boat . . . to drive away evil spirits. . . . A long time ago we were crossing [Lake Mille Lacs] in a steamboat. . . . The waves were so high that we thought we were going to drown. My great-grandfather threw three or four sacks of tobacco into the water and soon the waves took us back to [shore]."

Tobacco was believed to be a gift from the Great Spirit and was used for special occasions such as an invitation to a ceremony, formalizing a peace treaty, or forming a social bond.

way. The magic formed a great black cloud full of crashing rocks. These rocks caused lightning to strike. Little Turtle climbed on this cloud and was carried around the sky. She collected the lightning as she went. First she made it into a big ball and threw it into the sky and it became the sun. Then Little Turtle collected more lightning into a smaller ball, which became the moon.

Great Turtle commanded the animals to make holes in the corners of the sky so that the sun and moon could circle up and down across the sky. In this way, night and day were created.

The Manitous and the Midewiwin

The Algonquian-speaking tribes of the western Great Lakes region also believed in fabled spirits who inhabit the earth, watch over animals and growing things, and control the destinies of humans. The Ojibwa, Ottawa, Potawatomi, and related tribes called these spirits manitous. These tribes also believed in personal manitous, or guardians, who individuals acquired through fasting or dreaming. Upon death, it was believed that the soul of the human body followed manitous over a trail, past the Milky Way, to heaven in the West.

People of the Lakes describes the various places where Native Americans might find manitous:

The most remote of manitous were those that resided high up in the sky—the spirits of the male sun and the female moon and the four winds. . . . In the air below the domain of the highest manitous hovered the spirits of the birds, from the sacred eagle to the fearsome owl and the awe-inspiring thunderbird. That fabled being, which struck thunder from its wings and hurled lightning bolts from its talons, was not always dreaded. On earth dwelt the spirits that supervised the animals and either helped or hindered hunters, along with specific manitous that controlled harvests, presided over specific rituals or cures, or inhabited certain mysterious features such as strangely shaped rocks. At the lowest level—beneath the surface of lakes and rivers and beneath the floating island of earth itself—lurked the fearsome manitous that caused drowning, floods, and other misfortunes.[34]

Although some manitous were believed to cause sickness, the people of the western lakes, including the Sauk, Fox, Miami, Menominee, and Winnebago, believed they could reverse these evil spells. They formed a religious organization called the Midewiwin, or Grand Medicine Society, whose membership was restricted to men. Everyone knew about the Midewiwin, but the society's inner workings were supposed to be kept secret. The powers of this society were so great that many Native Americans believed that membership alone could cure sickness and grant the

Joining the Midewiwin

The Midewiwin, or Grand Medicine Society, was an organization devoted to healing the sick by religious means. George Irving Quimby writes in detail about the society in *Indian Life in the Upper Great Lakes.*

"The Society was divided into four grades or degrees taken in succession. Each degree required various ritual acts and a large payment. A Mide of the fourth degree was believed to possess a great supernatural power. Admission to membership in the Society was by dedication of a child at birth or by application. One might dream that he should join the Medicine Society. Applicants accepted by the Society were assigned to members for instructions in healing and religious ceremonies. Parts of the instructions and some ritual songs were recorded by means of pictures painted or incised on birchbark. . . .

[The] four degrees of membership [were] based upon an ascending order of complexity, skill, and prestige. Healing rites were also performed by lesser medicine men, or shamans, who were not members of the Midewiwin.

The Grand Medicine Society, clans, war parties, and certain individuals . . . possessed sacred medicine bundles—collections of magical paraphernalia held in woven bags or bags made from mink or otter skins and wrapped in small woven mats made especially for that purpose. Among the contents of the medicine bags were quartz crystals, fossils, shells, clusters of bird feathers, skins of special birds, effigy carvings, and all sorts of charms and amulets. On many different occasions there were religious rituals and ceremonies involving the use of sacred bundles."

soul eternal life. Practitioners of Midewiwin medicine could also engage in so-called bad medicine to bring great misfortune on other people, causing them to go insane or even die. Therefore, it was not surprising that many men, both sick and healthy, sought membership in the Midewiwin. Other less important medicine cults also existed that were composed of members who had shared a common vision or dream.

The power of the manitous and the spirits were embodied in sacred medicine bundles, and bags, charms, and other sacred objects. Rituals and ceremonies to bring about good medicine involved the music of drums, rattles, and whistles. These rituals also involved the eating of dogs that had been specially raised for the occasion. During the ceremonies dozens of stories were told that brought to life the power of the spirits and the manitous.

Naming Children

A Native American's spiritual journey was lifelong and even extended beyond his or her death. Native American children were guided at a very young age into the mysterious ways of the spirit world. The child's first formal contact with religious ritual was the naming ceremony. The parents of a baby asked a respected man or woman in the tribe to bestow a name upon the child that would also bring the blessings of the manitous that the elder was thought to possess. Often the names came to the elder in a dream.

When the child was about one month old, a ceremony was held that was attended by family members and their friends. The elder who would do the naming recounted all the blessings that he or she had enjoyed throughout life. It was this good fortune that the elder was giving the child through his or her name.

An Indian doctor concocts an herbal healing potion.

61

After announcing the name, a feast was held and formal prayers asked that the child enjoy long life and good health. Then the elder bestowed upon the child a gift that would be kept among the youngster's sacred possessions.

The ceremonial name was very spiritual and seldom used in daily life. Instead, the child used a nickname that emphasized some character trait or behavior. Anthropologist Mary Inez Hilger discusses the meaning of nicknames and quotes a member of the Ojibwa tribe as to their use:

[Affectionate] names were given to most small children, and as they grew older they received a nickname also. These were usually humorous: they might indicate a resemblance to some object or animal or be associated with an event that occurred during the first day of life. "I heard a little girl who was very spry called Grasshopper. Another was called Little Twig until she was old enough to know that it was not her real name." [35]

Growing Up with the Spirits

Native American children were generally treated indulgently and grew up believing that the spirits watched them constantly. The Ojibwa, for example, had taboos against hitting children or even harshly criticizing them. If children misbehaved, they were told stories of manitous or animals that might harm them. If youngsters wandered into a dangerous area of the forest, they might be chased off by a family member wearing a frightening mask. If children refused to quiet down at night, they would be warned that an owl would carry them off if they did not go to sleep.

Until the age of ten, children spent their time learning the skills of adulthood. Girls would care for dolls made from corn husks, and boys would practice hunting with tiny bows and arrows. When a boy killed his first animal, the entire family joined together in a celebratory feast.

When training children, little distinction was made by parents between the real world and the spirit world. All useful skills were said to come from the manitous. Stories of spirits and inspirational tales were told on long winter nights. One Ojibwa commented on this in *People of the Lakes:* "I have known some Indians . . . who could commence to relate legends and stories in the month of October and not end until quite late in the spring, and on every evening of this long term tell a new story." [36]

Vision Quests

While a child's parents provided stories of the spirit world, young people gained their own knowledge of the spirits through dreams. Children were encouraged to remember their dreams and speak of them. Since there were no schools or books, a great bulk of a young Native American's wisdom came from his or her dreams and the interpretation of them.

By the time young people reached puberty, they were anxious to seek out a vision or special dream that would in some way define their personality. This search was called a vision quest, and it was a common practice among people of the lakes as well as Native Americans elsewhere.

A vision quest was one of the deepest religious experiences in a Native American's entire life. As part of the quest, he or she had to give up food for a lengthy period. To prepare for a vision quest, children would practice short fasts even when they were very young. In *Chippewa Child Life,* a Native American recalls his first fast: "I fasted one day when I was 5 years old: I got no bread nor water nor any food all day. Those who fasted more than one day were usually permitted to drink, but not eat."[37] Learning to endure long fasts would later prove valuable for warriors, who fasted before battle, and for anyone who had to suffer through food shortages caused by crop failure or other misfortunes.

Children who were fasting colored their faces black with charcoal. In preparation for the vision quest, elders instructed the young and counseled them in how to interpret a vision. Examples were offered to the children of powerful visions as compared to dangerous or useless visions.

Timing of a vision quest was important. People believed that a quest carried out by a person too young to understand a vision was dangerous. On the other hand, it was

Coloring the face with charcoal signified that a child was fasting in preparation for a vision quest.

believed that those who waited too long risked becoming lazy for life. Because summer was a time when the call to the spirit world might be answered by an evil underwater manitou, vision quests were usually undertaken in the early spring or late fall.

Girls might venture out in search of a vision at any time, or their quest might correspond to the time of fasting and isolation performed during their first menstrual periods. Boys were expected to go on the quest before their voices started changing. After those events, which marked the beginning of puberty, children were considered too old to go on a vision quest.

Preparation

When the time was right, parents would escort their children to an isolated hilltop. Some built small lodges or a platform in a tree where the child would be assured of total isolation. There the youngster waited and fasted. A small amount of nourishment was only allowed after five days. After ten days, success was expected but not necessarily assured.

Girls were not expected to fast as long as boys, although some did. Boys were considered cowards if they could not fast for ten days. Although there were no records of anyone dying from such rigorous fasts, one older Native American relates, "I have known boys to fast until they could hardly stand on their legs."[38]

Children were urged not to ask too much from the vision, such as trying to see the Great Spirit for instance, who was believed to be unknowable. Children who fasted were believed to arouse the pity of the spirits and, in most cases, were granted a vision that would guide them through life. Children rarely spoke of their visions, however. A child might discuss it with his or her father or the tribe's medicine man, but to speak of a manitou vision to anyone else was not recommended.

If no vision was seen during the initial quest, the child would be expected to try and try again. If no vision ever appeared, the child was considered uninspired by other tribe members.

Over time some Native Americans have spoken of their visions, and the substance of them has been written down. Typically, a person on a vision quest would see a being who might take many forms—animal, human, or supernatural. The being offered compassion, insight, good fortune, and spiritual guidance. In *Chippewa Child Life,* anthropologist Hilger discusses the vision:

> The object which appears is adopted as the personal mystery, guardian spirit . . . of the entranced, and is never mentioned by him without first making a sacrifice. A small effigy of this [manitou] is carried suspended by a string around the neck, or if the wearer be a [Midewiwin] he carries it in his "medicine bag."[39]

After vision quests were over, children returned to their lodges for a celebration and a meal. Breaking the fast meant eating small amounts very slowly or else the child would become ill.

Huron Beliefs and Death Rituals

Along with vision quests and agricultural and hunting ceremonies, the people of the lakes performed many rituals concerning death and dying. Although these varied from tribe to tribe, the Huron had one of the most elaborate death rituals and beliefs. Their beliefs concerning death were recorded by George Irving Quimby in *Indian Life in the Upper Great Lakes:*

> The Hurons believed that dreams were the language of the soul. The soul, according to the Huron, had five aspects or conditions of being. It animated the body and gave it life. It was possessed of reason. It enabled thinking and deliberation. It made possible affection for others. And it separated itself from the body after death.[40]

The Huron tribe believed that after death souls went to villages in the sky. These villages were not associated with reward or punishment, as in the Christian version of heaven and hell, but were much like life on Earth. Huron souls followed the path of the Milky Way to the great soul village near the setting sun. Those who had died in war had their own separate village, as did the very old and the very young.

When a Huron died, his or her corpse was usually laid in a bark coffin atop raised wooden posts standing ten feet high. Infants, however, were buried along the roads between villages so that their souls could be born again by entering the bodies of women who walked past them. Likewise, people killed during wars were buried in shallow graves, and their souls were believed to remain in the vicinity of the Huron's earthly villages. None of these souls, however, journeyed to their respective villages in the sky until after an elaborate mass burial ceremony known as the Feast of the Dead. It was this ritual that most shocked the French Jesuit missionaries who first witnessed it in the early seventeenth century.

Every eight to twelve years, all of the bands of the Huron tribe gathered to hold the Feast of the Dead. In this national ceremony, the bodies of the dead were removed from their temporary graves to be buried in mass graves. Before the ceremony, tribe members carefully stripped the remaining flesh from the bones of the dead and threw the tissue in a fire. George Irving Quimby describes the next step in the process:

> After being stripped of flesh, the bones were placed in beaver-skin bags . . . or dressed in fine robes and adorned with bracelets and strings of beads. Some bags of bones were arranged to form human effigies that were ornamented with strings of beads and bands of long fur dyed red.

> At a place selected for burial, there was a large pit 30 feet to 60 feet square and up to 10 feet deep. At the edge of the pit was a high scaffold or platform. Bodies were hung from poles on this scaffold and bundles of bones were placed on the platform. After lengthy ceremonies and rituals in which the whole Huron nation participated, the bodies were placed in the pit along with the beautiful fur robes, pottery, weapons, tools, ornaments, food, and utensils.

Hundreds of people were thus buried and thousands of useful articles were lavished upon the dead. At the end of the Feast of the Dead the souls of the Hurons buried this way departed from Huronia and went to various soul villages in the sky.[41]

The people of the lakes carried out elaborate rituals for every aspect of life, from birth to death and even beyond. From the names of their babies to the herbs they harvested, the spirits, healing, and medicine of the Great Lakes tribes were as important to them as the air they breathed and the food they ate.

Chapter 5

War and Conflict

Native Americans in the Great Lakes region often engaged in wars between rival clans or tribes. As in most societies, these wars served as a means of acquiring territory, controlling trade, and gaining respect and prestige.

Warfare was a way of life for the Iroquois and other Great Lakes tribes. Since the power and status of warriors increased with each battle, war—and the glory it brought—was a major part of Native American culture. The Iroquois made war on enemies and even upon neighboring clans. After a war party attacked a nearby village, reprisals would result, followed by revenge and years of blood feud. This resulted in fear and hatred among the tribes of the Iroquois Nation.

Intertribal wars often began when a man in one tribe murdered members of a rival tribe. When this happened, the wronged tribe would seek to take prisoners to compensate for the earlier loss. Sometimes these conflicts grew extremely bitter and lasted for generations.

Native American Ways of War

Warfare techniques practiced by Native Americans of the Great Lakes differed little whether among members of the Iroquois Nation or the Algonquians. A typical war raid in Iroquois country, for example, might be instigated by relatives of a person slain by an enemy tribe. Although tribes had different chiefs with different duties, it was the job of the war chief to declare that retribution was necessary. The war chief might make such a declaration at the victim's funeral. The chief then sought volunteers for a war party from his village and neighboring villages. Younger men who desired to prove their bravery were the most eager volunteers.

Several hundred men or more might be gathered when a war party was assembled. War chiefs called the men to council, and a feast was held. Women served platters of dog meat, which symbolized the flesh and blood of enemy prisoners who would be captured. After the meal, dancing and singing filled the night as warriors beat on drums, shook rattles, and danced using the motions of a ritual battle. Tobacco offerings were made to the war spirits, and prayers were offered for a safe return of the warriors. Shamans were asked to peer into the future and predict the outcome of the raid.

Once the war party entered enemy territory, it might break up into five or six groups of thirty to forty men each. When the war parties were met by a large number of enemy warriors, bows were drawn on both sides and arrows rained down on the assembled warriors from a distance. After the initial skirmish, the men moved in for close combat, wielding ball-headed war clubs. Acts of insolent bravery were highly valued on the battlefield. The most audacious act was to humiliate one's opponent by simply hitting him with a special stick. This act, sometimes called "counting coup," was described in *America's Fascinating Indian Heritage:* "To dart through a phalanx of foe to touch an enemy war leader with a hand or stick was the ultimate in courage. The brave who had shown such daring was rewarded with the highest honor, a new name, chosen by the commander of the expedition."[42]

In some cases, the raiders sneaked up on people working in fields or hunting and either killed and scalped them or took them prisoner. When the war parties returned to their villages, they let out special whoops or cries to let people know whether they had been successful.

Taking Prisoners

When prisoners were taken, they were turned over to the war chiefs, who decided what should be done with them. Women and children were usually adopted by families to replace lost relatives. Male prisoners had a more uncertain future. Depending on the whim of the chief, men could be kept as part of a family or condemned to torture and death. The horrible torture ceremonies are recounted in *Realm of the Iroquois:*

> If a prisoner's demeanor or abilities pleased his guardians, they might choose to let him live and become part of their family. A prisoner condemned to die, however, was also formally adopted by his captors, who addressed him as "brother" or "nephew" and spoke words of affection to him even as they prepared him for his terrible fate. The women wept when they fed him, and the men shared their tobacco pipe with him and wiped the sweat from his face.

> The torture ceremony, which could last several days, began with a farewell feast, during which the prisoner sang songs and showed his courage by walking up and down the longhouse, inviting his captors to kill him. Prisoners always looked for opportunities to flee—some were forced to walk on live coals as part of their ordeal and took the occasion to kick the embers aside,

starting fires or raising smoke that gave them a slim chance to escape. Barring that, they behaved as bravely as possible throughout the gruesome event, knowing it reflected well on their people and frustrated their tormentors; the Iroquois considered it an evil omen if their victims failed to weep and beg for mercy. Such stoicism must have been extremely difficult to sustain, however, for the torture was both grisly and unrelenting. Prisoners had their fingernails torn out, their bones broken, and their ears pierced with burning sticks. They received scalding burns and deep cuts on all parts of their bodies. The tormentors, both men and women, mocked them continuously throughout the ceremony, trying to get them to break down.[43]

Many times the prisoners would survive this ordeal. At the final execution, further torments were visited on the victim before he was mercifully killed by a club to the head. If the prisoner had proven

Victory Celebrations

When a war party returned from a victorious raid, a celebration called a *misekwe,* or "scalp dance," was held. The celebration and its significance to the warriors are detailed in *America's Fascinating Indian Heritage.*

"After the scalps were all collected, the dance began, and as each warrior circled the lodge, he lifted his voice in a chant that recounted his feats on the battlefield. 'In this manner I clubbed him down,' one might sing while chopping at the air. 'He cried out and begged for mercy, but I had no pity for him!' Though this kind of self-praise was encouraged, exaggeration was scorned. A man who embroidered his account with fictional acts of valor was disgraced and viewed with contempt by his fellow warriors.

During the scalp dance each of the braves flourished his sacred war bundle, which was carried into every encounter. The bundle, made of animal skin, contained such charms and relics as tangles of weasel fur, a buffalo horn, rattlesnake rattles, and a string of human scalps. This pouch, symbolic of past victories and the ancestry of the warrior, was thought to have magical powers that protected the owner from harm. The pouch, a breechclout, and leggings were all the warriors wore into battle. All other clothes were left behind, for these were infused not only with their owner's own spirit but with the spirit of his tribe as well. Should the garments be captured and abused by an enemy, the entire tribe might suffer disaster."

exceptionally brave, young warriors would roast and eat his heart, hoping to gain some of his courage in the process.

Ordeals suffered by prisoners naturally provoked calls for retaliation by the victim's friends and family and led to years of feuding. Before the formation of the Iroquois League, for example, blood feuds, cannibalism, and brutality often set clan against clan. Archaeologists believe the violence reached its peak around the year 1500. During this period of warfare, tribes tried to form alliances with some tribes while battling others.

Warfare was sometimes prevented when a tribe served as a buffer between competing groups. In the early 1600s, for example, the Huron were employed in peaceful trading with various Algonquian tribes while engaged in bitter fighting with the Iroquois Nation. In the mid-1600s, the Huron homeland was overrun by the Iroquois. The surviving Huron fled westward to live among the central Algonquian tribes.

The Algonquian, for their part, had their own rivalries. The Menominee and the Winnebago tribes battled the Sauk and the Fox, who in turn fought with the Ojibwa. But none of the warring tribes could imagine the changes they were about to face when a new group of men arrived one day on their shores looking for fur pelts.

The Europeans Arrive

In the first half of the seventeenth century, boats and canoes began to sail into the Great Lakes carrying white men who, unlike the smooth-skinned Native Americans, had bearded faces. These "hairy faces" did not come to conquer the place they called New France, or the New World, but to trade with the people they called savages.

In what is now the Canadian province of Quebec, the French arrived eager to obtain animal furs. Farther south, newcomers arrived from England, Holland, Sweden, and Germany. Their motivations in the New World ranged from obtaining religious freedom to searching for gold. There was no gold to be found, so those who survived the harsh winters settled down to become farmers and fishermen.

At first, contact between whites and Native Americans was beneficial for all. The people of the lakes were eager to obtain the Europeans' muskets—smoking, death-dealing weapons that the Native Americans at first thought were magical. In addition to firearms, white traders offered fishhooks, brass kettles, metal knives, axes, sewing needles, and other goods that made daily life easier for the Native Americans.

The Native Americans, for their part, showed the Europeans how to survive in the wilderness surrounding the Great Lakes. The newcomers were introduced to corn, pumpkin, and edible berries and nuts. In addition, the skilled Indian hunters showed the whites how to hunt game in the forests. This period of friendship, however, would not last long.

Many of the Europeans wanted land— land that could be fenced, plowed, tim-

Europeans and Native Americans benefited from each other. The Native Americans taught the whites how to survive, while they traded for firearms, fishhooks, brass kettles, knives, axes, and sewing needles.

bered, mined, and exclusively owned by one person and passed on to that person's descendants. Native Americans did not believe that a person could own land. They believed instead that the kind spirits of the earth simply allowed people to live there. Meanwhile, European kings who had never seen the so-called New World gave away huge parcels of Native American land to business associates—land upon which the Europeans had no legal or moral claims.

Native Americans at first did not see a problem with this new turn of events, and as long as the white men were few in number and did not encroach on their hunting grounds, there was relatively little trouble between the two races. Each year, however, more and more European settlements were established and grew. Native Americans were faced with the choice of giving in to the whites' demands for territory or suffering destruction.

Changing Tradition with Trade Goods

European trade goods were both a blessing and a curse to the Native Americans in the Great Lakes region. When they first encountered explorer Samuel de Champlain in 1609, members of the Huron tribe were amazed by the European items offered to them by the French explorer. Within twenty or thirty years, however, these goods, especially those made of metal, had become necessities and encouraged a fundamental change of life.

When the Huron tribespeople accepted new items, such as iron pots, knives, and weapons, into their culture, they began to lose the skills needed to make items necessary for daily life from traditional methods and materials. Within seventy-five years, no one among the Huron remembered how to manufacture needed items from wood or stone. Because of their dependence on European goods, members of the Huron tribe were forced to depend on the fur trade to sustain their tribe. Due to heavy trapping, however, furbearing animals such as the beaver virtually disappeared in Huronia. This drove the Huron into hunting grounds claimed by other tribes, increasing competition and hostility that eventually led to the total destruction of the Huron people in the region.

French Fur Traders

The first Europeans in the Great Lakes region were French fur traders, and their leader was Samuel de Champlain. In 1608 Champlain and a small party of men sailed up the St. Lawrence River in search of beaver pelts. The next spring Champlain made first contact with the Algonquin tribe, whose altered name, Algonquian, would come to refer to a host of linguistically and culturally related tribes. Although thousands of native people lived in the area, Champlain claimed the lands for France and began renaming rivers, lakes, and geographical features with French names.

Almost as soon as the white men arrived in the region, they began to alter the relationships between the tribes. Some clans were given muskets in trade for furs while others were ignored. The contact with Europeans forever changed the balance of power among Native American tribes.

To gain the favor of the Algonquin tribespeople, Champlain helped them in a raid against their traditional foes, the Mohawk of the Iroquois League. Thanks to the French-supplied muskets, the Algonquin people found easy victory against the bow-and-arrow wielding Mohawk.

Champlain's actions made the well-organized tribes of the Iroquois League permanent enemies of France. In the eighteenth century, this fact would not bode well for French claims in the New World. When France and Great Britain battled for dominance over the North

American continent, the Iroquois steadfastly sided with the British.

Champlain went back to France shortly after the Algonquin victory, but he returned to the New World seven years later. In 1615 he pushed far west into the lands of the Huron tribe. Although Iroquois themselves, the Huron Indians were nonetheless enemies of the members of the Iroquois League. Champlain was convinced that the industrious Huron tribe would make a great trading partner for New France because of the tribe's strategic location between two of the Great Lakes, Erie and Huron. Before long members of the Huron tribe were acting as middlemen in the fur trade, channeling thousands of beaver pelts into the hands of the French from the eastern, western, and northern Algonquian tribes. The Huron became greatly enriched, but the long-smoldering hostilities between the Huron and the Iroquois quickly burst into flame.

While the Huron worked with the French, the Iroquois made alliances with the fur-seeking Dutch. In 1648, well-armed with Dutch muskets, the tribes of the Iroquois League attacked the less aggressive Huron. The Iroquois warriors launched a two-day offensive against the Huron and slaughtered all who did not escape into the forest. Villages were pillaged and burned. Those who survived the onslaught fled farther west and north; others surrendered to the enemy and were adopted into the Iroquois League.

The Iroquois pressed on from one village to the next, crushing a large clan

In his search for beaver pelts, Samuel de Champlain sailed up the St. Lawrence River, claiming land and renaming rivers and lakes with French names.

73

Disease Epidemics

European traders brought the Native Americans more than just trade goods; they also brought a host of deadly diseases to which the people of the lakes had no immunity. Descriptions of epidemics among the Native Americans are found in reports from European settlers, soldiers, and missionaries. Reports vary in accuracy, though. Some name a specific disease such as measles, cholera, or smallpox. Other reports, however, merely describe the epidemics as "distemper," "rashes," or "fevers" that proved fatal to the Native Americans.

Although these diseases also killed white people, Native Americans had little resistance to these diseases and were much more severely affected by them. Deadly illnesses included scarlet fever, diphtheria, yellow fever, typhoid fever, meningitis, whooping cough, influenza, and dysentery. Epidemics devastated the populations, sometimes killing half to three-quarters of all inhabitants of a Native American village. The diseases were spread when people moved out of affected villages and into other locations. Sometimes Europeans, who were eager to elimi-

nate their Native American enemies, purposely gave their foes smallpox-infected blankets in order to spread the disease among the tribes.

The first smallpox outbreak occurred among the Seneca in 1633 and 1634. A series of contagious diseases decimated the Huron tribe beginning in 1634. By 1637 scarlet fever had wiped out dozens of Mohawk clans. Epidemics among the Winnebago in Wisconsin killed twenty thousand between 1634 and 1670, leaving only six hundred surviving members of the tribe.

By the eighteenth century, the epidemics wiped out the Miami and Illinois tribes. Between 1833 and 1846 diseases reduced the numbers of Sauk and Fox tribespeople from six thousand to twenty-four hundred. By 1870 more than twenty-six hundred of the four thousand members of the Menominee tribe had been killed. By the beginning of the twentieth century, the deadly European diseases had killed more than two-thirds of the once-thriving community of Native Americans in the Great Lakes region.

called the Tobacco Huron. By the end of 1649, the survivors of the Huron Nation were near mass starvation. Epidemics spread among the already weakened people. The cornfields of the Huron were grown over by weeds, and the winds blew through hundreds of rotting longhouses

that had once sheltered thirty thousand Huron. The once mighty Huron Nation was laid to waste.

The Era of the English

With the defeat of the Huron tribe, the Iroquois League gained control of the Great

Lakes fur trade. This created conflict between the English and the French fur traders, who both scrambled for their share of each year's harvest of pelts. But while the French had come to the New World mostly for furs, the English had come for land.

By the eighteenth century, the eastern coast of America was lined with cities, villages, and towns. Large cities such as Boston, New York, and Richmond were part of a burgeoning trade with Europe that included fish, timber, minerals, and farm products taken from territory once occupied by Native Americans.

In 1722 the Tuscarora tribe migrated into Iroquois country after being pushed out of North Carolina by English settlers. The Tuscarora became the sixth nation in the Iroquois League. By this time, Iroquois power extended as far west as Ojibwa country and as far south as the colony of Georgia. But soon enough, even the power of the Iroquois Nation would be challenged.

With their East Coast settlements secure, the English began to push inland, sowing new fields, building new cities, and evicting the local Native Americans. Whites were not the only people who were invading Indian lands, though. After a series of defeats in wars against the whites, survivors of East Coast tribes also began to move west into the Great Lakes region.

Unlike the French, who depended on the original inhabitants to trap beavers, the English had no interest in preserving Native American society. Instead, Native Americans were considered hindrances to progress—hindrances that needed to be destroyed. In the end, however, it was not the English who would pose the greatest problem for Native Americans of the Great Lakes.

When East Coast settlements began to develop into villages, towns, and cities, more and more land was taken away from the Native Americans.

In a series of wars fought between England and France in the seventeenth and eighteenth centuries, the Iroquois generally joined forces with the English while the Algonquian tribes sided with the French. When the British finally defeated the French in 1760, a lasting peace seemed possible. But in 1775, the American col-

Beaver Hats

By the end of the 1600s, thousands of white men were pouring into the Great Lakes region. Many of them made their living from one simple item: the beaver hat. From the seventeenth century until the middle of the nineteenth century, no proper European gentleman would appear in public without one. Fur trappers and hatters could barely keep up with the demand. In 1760 alone, the Hudson Bay Company—located on former Iroquois land—exported enough beaver pelts to England to make 576,000 hats.

In addition to beavers, trappers exported pelts—called "brown gold"—from marten, foxes, otters, panthers, bears, deer, and other furbearing animals. These were turned into collars, gloves, decorative hems, sleeves, and boots for men and women.

By the 1800s excessive hunting had wiped out the beaver and many other animals in the Great Lakes region. At that point, trappers moved farther west and began the process all over again in the Rocky Mountain region.

Variations of the Beaver Hat

A clerical hat
(Eighteenth century)

The continental cocked hat
(1776)

The Wellington
(1812)

The Paris beau
(1815)

The D'orsay
(1820)

The regent
(1825)

The demand for beaver hats led to the near extinction of the beaver in the Great Lakes area by the 1800s.

This British cartoon shows the Iroquois siding with the English during the war between England and France.

onists began a revolution against British rule and expelled the English from what would, in just a few years, be the United States of America.

Unfortunately for the Iroquois, four of the six tribes of the Iroquois League sided with the British in the Revolutionary War. A Mohawk chief whom the whites called Joseph Brant had been made a captain by the British. Hundreds of Iroquois warriors and British guerrillas marching with Brant laid waste to American settlements in western New York and Pennsylvania. In retaliation, George Washington, commander in chief of the American army, sent a force under General John Sullivan to rout the Native Americans. Sullivan led a campaign of pillage and arson that destroyed forty Iroquois villages and most of their crops. Reduced to starvation, the Iroquois saw the last vestige of their power obliterated.

When a peace treaty ending the American Revolution was signed in 1783, Great Britain ceded to America most of the vast territory that stretched from the East Coast to the Mississippi River. Within these vast forests were the homelands of the Miami, Ottawa, Menominee, Illinois, Potawatomi, Ojibwa, Sauk, Fox, and Winnebago tribes. Soon these tribes, like the Iroquois, would have to confront the white people's land

During the Revolutionary War, Mohawk chief Joseph Brant was made a captain by the British and led his warriors to destroy many American settlements.

traders who bartered—and sometimes fought—with British and Canadian fur traders who had long-established trade relations with Native Americans in the area. The fur traders brought alcohol to the Native Americans, who at first believed that it was a magical potion that could inspire much-sought-after dreams. Next to smallpox and other epidemics, alcohol proved by far to be the most destructive force to the Native Americans, who would gladly trade an entire season's worth of pelts for two or three bottles of rum.

Whiskey and rum became the white people's main weapon in subjugating the Native Americans in order to seize their lands. The U.S. Army and scores of "Indian agents" poured into the Northwest Territory. These people used every means possible—including liquor, flattery, coercion, and threats of force—to induce Native Americans to give up vast stretches of their domain.

hunger as well as their diseases. Step by step, they would be forced from the lands as their way of life was pushed into oblivion.

Living in the United States

Early in the nineteenth century, the area around the southern Great Lakes was known to white people in the United States as the Northwest Territory. The first Americans to arrive in this region were fur

Chiefs, or men the white men called chiefs, were wined and dined in order to get their signatures on treaties that opened Native American lands to white settlements. These tribesmen could neither read nor write and thus had no way to understand the complicated legal language of the treaties. In addition, the so-called chiefs rarely had the authority to make decisions on behalf of their tribes, but the whites chose to take their signatures as legal title to the lands. If their fellow tribesmen resisted, military force was used to enforce the treaties.

The Fate of the Sauk and Fox Tribes

The fate of the Sauk and the Fox is characteristic of the problems faced by all of the Great Lakes tribes. During the seventeenth and eighteenth centuries, the Sauk and the Fox relocated several times as their territory east of Lake Michigan was invaded by whites and by eastern tribes fleeing west. In 1804 chiefs of the Sauk

and Fox tribes were ordered to St. Louis by federal agents. The chiefs were plied with alcohol and forced to sign an agreement to cede all of their tribal lands east of the Mississippi River in Illinois, Wisconsin, and Missouri.

For this territory, the Sauk were awarded six hundred dollars a year for an unspecified number of years; the Fox were awarded four hundred dollars a year. The four Sauk delegates who signed the treaty received clothing and other items worth about two thousand dollars—a considerable sum at the time. The terms of the treaty stated that the tribes could stay on

Whiskey and rum became so popular among Native Americans that they would sometimes trade an entire season's worth of pelts for two or three bottles.

the land until the U.S. government sold it to settlers. The other members of the tribes were angry when they heard of the treaty and said the four men who signed it did not represent them.

As the years passed, more and more white settlers moved to the area, and small skirmishes erupted between whites and Native Americans. In 1829 the federal government decided to sell all of the lands covered in the 1804 treaty. Nearly all of the Fox tribespeople, and many of the Sauk, decided to move west of the Mississippi River into Iowa. Some of the Sauk, however, refused to leave their homeland, the center of which was the village of Saukenuk, located between the Mississippi and Rock Rivers.

In the spring of 1830, the Sauk returned from a winter hunting expedition to find American settlers living in Saukenuk. The Americans were occupying Sauk longhouses and planting crops in Sauk cornfields. At that time, a forty-eight-year-old Sauk leader named Black Hawk protested to the U.S. Indian agent in the region. Black Hawk describes the dispute in his autobiography:

We acquainted our agent daily with our situation . . . and hoped that something would be done for us. The whites were *complaining* at the same time that *we* were *intruding* upon *their rights!* THEY made themselves the *injured* party, and *we* the *intruders!* and called loudly to the great war chief to protect *their* property!

How smooth must be the language of the whites, when they can make right look like wrong, and wrong like right.[44]

The terms of the treaty that the Sauk were forced to sign provided that they could stay on their land only until the U.S. government sold it to settlers.

Black Hawk's War

The military forced the Sauk to leave their homeland, but they did not stay away for long. In 1831 about five hundred Sauk and Fox men and women rallied around Black Hawk, who promised to regain the rights to their ancestral lands. Black Hawk also enlisted the help of the Winnebago and Potawatomi. That spring, the Sauk returned to Saukenuk. For reasons that are unclear, Black Hawk believed that he could convince the settlers to peacefully leave the Sauk land. John Reynolds, the governor of Illinois at the time, called the action an invasion of the United States. He called out seven hundred militiamen and said the Sauk should be removed dead or alive. The Sauk fled in the middle of the night and escaped to Iowa. With no provisions, the Native Americans were forced to subsist for weeks on wild roots and grasses.

Black Hawk enlisted the help of the Winnebago and Potawatomi to regain the rights to their ancestral lands.

Black Hawk realized that his mission was a lost cause and made haste to negotiate peace. But when eight Sauk men, waving a white flag approached a group of soldiers, the Americans panicked and fired on the Native Americans, killing four of them. This action enraged a group of forty Sauk warriors who waited nearby. They attacked the American soldiers, killing some and frightening off the rest.

The crisis worsened as infuriated settlers joined a two-thousand-member militia. When President Andrew Jackson learned of the situation, he ordered the military to capture Black Hawk and his followers. The Sauk tribespeople continued their trek into Iowa, hoping that if they retreated they would be left in peace. Jackson, however, ordered the army to pursue and attack the retreating Native Americans. On July 21, 1832, soldiers murdered seventy Sauk men, women, and children on an island in the Wisconsin River.

On August 1 Black Hawk attempted another surrender. This time forty members of the Sauk tribe were killed by soldiers in a heavy barrage of gunfire. Two days later, the army launched a full-scale assault on the Sauk encampment. In more than eight hours of gunfire, some two hundred men, women, and children were slaughtered in-

Native American Land Cessions

The treaty-making procedure that the United States used to acquire Native American lands is called a land "cession" in the United States and a land "surrender" in Canada. By 1873 most land in the Great Lakes region had been taken from the natives by about 130 American treaties and 27 Canadian treaties. Only small portions of the province of Ontario around Lake Simco and the Red Lake region of northern Minnesota were still under Native American jurisdiction.

Many of the cessions or surrenders fell into three historical periods. Between 1793 and 1805, after the Revolutionary War, Americans who had remained loyal to England immigrated to Canada. Canadian officials secured land for them in surrenders from the Iroquois on the upper shores of the St. Lawrence River and along the north shores of Lakes Ontario and Erie.

After independence, the 1795 Treaty of Greenville ceded two-thirds of the modern-day state of Ohio; parts of Michigan, Illinois, and Indiana; and opened up land for white settlement along the southern coast of Lake Erie. At this time both the Canadian and the U.S. government also assumed control over waterways deemed strategic for military purposes, taking away Native American control of thousands of miles of river and lake shoreline.

The next major land cessions occurred between 1815 and 1836. Treaties in the Illinois Territory between 1817 and 1821 confiscated lands from the Sauk, Fox, and Kickapoo tribes. Between 1824 and 1837, in the wake of Black Hawk's defeat, lands were ceded by the Potawatomi, Winnebago, Menominee, and Sauk in Illinois and Wisconsin.

The last land cessions occurred between 1842 and 1872. Mining, lumber, and railroad interests were mainly served by the government's acquisition of lands in the northwest sectors of the Great Lakes region. In Minnesota, Iowa, and the Dakota Territories, lands were taken from the Ojibwa, Sauk, and Fox tribes as well as from other Great Plains tribes farther west.

discriminately. Women were shot or drowned as they attempted to swim in the Mississippi River with their children on their backs.

The survivors of the massacre resumed their journey to Iowa. This was the end of the short-lived conflict known as Black Hawk's War. Black Hawk surrendered to government officials and was imprisoned for a short time. He later settled in a Sauk village on the Des Moines River. Years later, Black Hawk wrote about the events that had been so costly for his tribe:

On the way down [to the military prison] I surveyed the country that had cost us so much trouble, anxiety, and blood, and that now caused me to be a prisoner of war. I reflected upon the ingratitude of the whites, when I saw their fine houses, rich harvests, and everything desirable around them; and recollected that all this land had been ours, for which me and my people never received a dollar, and that the whites were not satisfied until they took our village and our grave-yards from us, and removed us across the Mississippi.[45]

The Final Removal

Black Hawk's War marked the end of the tribal dominance of the Great Lakes region. When the fate of the Sauk became known to other tribes, the tribes hastened to make peace with the United States. In 1835 the Ojibwa, Menominee, Iowa, Winnebago, Ottawa, and Potawatomi tribes signed treaties allowing the United States to make peaceful, final adjustments to Native American land claims.

By the 1850s the adjustments had been made, and the tribes were confined to tiny reservations within their ancient homelands where there was often not enough game to support them. Other Native Americans were driven to the harsh, dry territories in rural Oklahoma, Kansas, and other plains states where farming and hunting was all but impossible for people accustomed to the Great Lakes woodlands.

The wild lands of the Great Lakes region quickly began to fill with farms, factories, roads, towns, and cities. The once free people of the lakes now owed their very existence on reservations to welfare from the U.S. government—the same government that had taken their lands by force.

Chapter 6

People of the Lakes Today

Some of the tribes who had inhabited the shores of the Great Lakes for thousands of years have since been lost to history, and their culture with them. But a great deal of Native American culture has survived and is being rediscovered, revived, and put to use at the dawn of the twenty-first century.

The modern population of Native Americans in the United States is changing and growing. According to the U.S. Census Bureau, in the 1990s about 2 million people who identified themselves as Native Americans were living in the United States—up from 1.4 million in 1980 and the all-time low of 248,000 in 1890. But according to Edna L. Paisano at the U.S. Census Bureau,

The 72 percent increase between the 1970 and 1980 censuses and the 38 percent increase between the 1980 and 1990 censuses cannot be attributed only to natural increase. Other factors that may have contributed to the higher count of American Indi-

ans include improvements in the question [on the census form] on race; improvements in the way the Census Bureau counted people on reservations, on trust lands, and in Alaska Native villages; continued use of self-identification to obtain information on race; a greater propensity in 1990 than in earlier censuses for individuals (especially those of mixed Indian and non-Indian parentage) to report themselves as American Indian; and improved outreach programs and promotion campaigns.[46]

While most Native Americans live west of the Mississippi River, over 110,000 Native Americans of the Great Lakes region live either full or part time on reservations in New York, Michigan, Wisconsin, and Minnesota. Another 150,000 live away from the reservations or on reservations in other states. In addition, about 170,000 indigenous people live in the Great Lakes regions of Canada.

After years of failed government programs that attempted to help, change, or assimilate Native Americans, statistics for this segment of American society still look grim. Native American health, education, and income statistics are among the worst in the country. According to the National Indian Gaming Association,

> Indians, the first Americans, make up only one-half of 1 percent of the entire United States population. This makes them the smallest minority in the U.S. Those living on reservations are still at the bottom of virtually every economic category.

Unemployment rates often reach ten times the national average on reservations, many of which are located on remote lands that no one else wants, with little or no tax base. The life expectancy of the American Indian is 47 years, contrasted with the American average of 78.

The 1990 U.S. Census revealed that 30.9 percent of the country's Indians live in poverty. Their poverty rate is the highest of any ethnic group in America. The census defines poverty as an individual earning less than $6,300 a year, or a family of four earning less than $12,674. The poverty rate for the entire United States population was much lower, 13.1 percent.

Sovereign Native American Nations

In 1795 Native Americans ceded two-thirds of the Ohio Territory to the U.S. government by signing the Greenville treaty. This agreement forced Native Americans onto reservations around the southern shores of the Great Lakes, but it also recognized the Native American tribes as sovereign entities, somewhat like foreign countries located within the United States. Editors of Time-Life Books elaborate on U.S.–Native American treaties in the book *The Reservations*.

"The Greenville Treaty and others . . . were based on an assumption that bedevils the courts to this day. In theory, the federal government recognized the sovereignty of Indian tribes and negotiated treaties with them . . . as if they were foreign nations. In reality, government negotiators frequently employed threats, military force, bribery, or guile to win the signatures of Indian leaders who frequently did not fully understand the English-language documents and they were often unaware that they were signing away their land. . . . Yet the fact that the U.S. negotiators accepted the tribes as legal equals at the time allows modern Indians to legitimately claim that their treaty-recognized domains are a kind of sovereign state and thus deserving of special prerogatives under American law—an argument that remains at the heart of Indian public life today."

Over 110,000 Native Americans in the Great Lakes region live on reservations.

The unemployment rate for all Indians living on reservations was 45 percent in 1991, according to latest figures available from the Bureau of Indian Affairs. Some tribes have unemployment rates as high as 80%. An unemployment rate of more than 6% in a community in Mainstream America is considered a recession; and a rate of 9% is a depression. But even this number does not tell the whole story. Of those Indians who had jobs, only 28 percent earned more than $7,000 a year, according to the Bureau of Indian Affairs.[47]

The twentieth century has not been an easy one for the original people of the lakes. But like people everywhere, they have adjusted and changed to live in the modern world while trying to preserve the culture of their ancestors.

The Iroquois Today

During the nineteenth century, the Mohawk tribe made a transition from female-practiced to male-practiced agriculture. It moved out of its female-owned longhouses and into male-owned single-family dwellings. Tribespeople who survived the wars and disease moved to the St. Regis Mohawk

Reservation located in New York State and in Canada's Ontario and Quebec provinces.

In the 1920s and 1930s a Seneca chief named Handsome Lake revived the old female–hereditary system of chiefs in what is known as the Longhouse religion. Today, three tribes in New York—the Onondaga, Tonawanda, and Tuscarora—are governed by the old system in which clan mothers nominate their male chiefs.

Over the years other members of the Iroquois League have moved to reservations in Wisconsin and Oklahoma. Regardless of where they live, these reser-

vation Indians live much the same as their rural non–Native American neighbors. They maintain vegetable gardens and farm, and some go to college or work at factory or construction jobs when they can find them.

During the last half of the twentieth century, the Iroquois were forced to forfeit more land to the U.S. government when the St. Lawrence Seaway was expanded in the mid-1950s. Although the Native Americans tried to stop the project—taking their case all the way to the U.S. Supreme Court—the construction went ahead as planned.

The High-Steel Mohawk

Some members of the Mohawk tribe are particularly noted as ironworkers who travel about the United States and Canada constructing skyscrapers and bridges. The first Mohawk tribespeople to build bridges were hired in 1886 by the Canadian Pacific Railroad to construct an iron bridge across the St. Lawrence River near Montreal. The south end of the span rested on Mohawk land, and to obtain permission to build there, the Dominion Bridge Company agreed to hire Mohawk workers for the job. The results astounded the white owners of the company, who claimed the Mohawk were natural-born bridgemen.

The reputation of Mohawk ironworkers spread, and within a year fifty Mohawk workers were hired to build the Sault Sainte Marie Bridge in northern Michigan. Al-

though the wages were good, the work was dangerous and scores of Mohawk workers died in their first decade of ironworking.

In the twentieth century, the Mohawk made the transition from constructing bridges to erecting skyscrapers. Mohawk ironworkers helped build almost all of New York City's original skyscrapers, including the RCA Building, Rockefeller Center, and the quarter-mile-high Empire State Building. In 1957 about eight hundred Mohawk tribespeople were living and working in the city.

Today, the Mohawk and other Iroquois continue their high-steel tradition. They work on skyscrapers across the country and take pride in their difficult and dangerous career, echoing the brave ways of their warrior ancestors.

Robbie Robertson's Music for Native Americans

Robbie Robertson was born in Canada in 1943. He became famous in the mid-1960s as a lead guitarist for singer Bob Dylan. In the 1970s he was in the popular rock group known as the Band, writing songs like "The Weight" and "The Night They Drove Old Dixie Down." In the 1990s Robertson returned to his Mohawk roots with a compact disc entitled *Music for the Native Americans,* which he recorded with the Red Road Ensemble, a Native American group. With songs such as "Heartbeat Drum Song" and "Golden Feather," Robertson combines the intricate textures of Native American song and dance with modern rock that has its roots in both old blues and new electronic programming. Most of the performers, including Robertson, have some Native American ancestry.

Robertson's 1998 album, *From the Underworld of Redboy,* is even more focused on the musician's Iroquois heritage and features songs such as "The Code of Handsome Lake." In 1999 *Redboy* was nominated for two Grammy Awards. Ironically, although the album is by and about Native Americans, it was nominated in the category of "world music."

Returning to his Mohawk Indian roots, Robbie Robertson recorded a CD with the Red Road Ensemble, a Native American group.

In 1959, as the St. Lawrence Seaway project was getting underway, the New York Power Authority appropriated a sizable portion of the Tuscarora reservation near Niagara Falls for a hydroelectric project on the Niagara River. Members of the tribe protested by lying down in front of bulldozers. Their demonstration prevented work on the dam until the land seizure was reduced.

In western New York around the same time, the U.S. Army Corps of Engineers proposed to build a dam on the Allegheny River. The dam would flood nine thousand acres of the Allegany Indian Reservation, where the Seneca tribe had lived since 1794. This project threatened to submerge the village where Handsome Lake had revived the ancient Longhouse religion in the 1920s. The Seneca lost their fight, and the birthplace of the Longhouse religion vanished under the man-made lake.

In spite of the setbacks, the sovereign Iroquois Nation has endured. Today about fifty-five thousand descendants of the old league are scattered across sixteen reservations in New York, Wisconsin, Oklahoma, Ontario, and Quebec. The tribes continue to share a collective conviction that the original Iroquois Nation composed the first union of American states. Whenever the Iroquois come together to honor their traditions of peace and power, the spirit of the Iroquois Nation continues to grow.

The Huron and Wyandot Today

The modern Huron and Wyandot tribes live much like their non-Indian neighbors in Canada and America. But in recent years, many of the tribe members have enjoyed a revival of their traditions and have taken new pride in their important role in the history of the Great Lakes region.

During the first half of the twentieth century, the Huron reservation at Wendake in Quebec decreased in size and population as more and more Huron tribespeople left to live in towns and cities. The tribe sold much of its land to non–Native Americans. Other portions of the reservation were confiscated in the 1960s by the Canadian government for the creation of parks and the construction of a railroad. In 1968 Huron leaders convinced the Canadian government to return some territory to them and were rewarded with 143 acres adjacent to the Wendake reservation.

Visitors to the older part of the reservation today will see narrow streets lined with shops that sell native handicrafts such as baskets and embroidered cloth. Reservation factories manufacture about fifty thousand pairs of snowshoes and three thousand canvas canoes per year for sale throughout North America. The newer part of the reservation, with its modern houses and tree-lined streets reflects the economic prosperity of the tribe that has the highest standard of living of all Canadian reservations.

Residents of the Wendake reservation have a variety of ways of supporting themselves. Some work in the reservation shops, own small businesses, or commute to nearby towns to work. About twenty-five hundred Huron tribespeople survive in Canada today, about half on the reservation.

Unlike their Canadian relatives, about 3,500 members of the Wyandot tribe in the United States do not live on a reservation. They do, however, maintain a 188-acre tract of land near the small town of Wyandotte, Oklahoma. About 350 people live on this land and another 500 live nearby.

Members of the Wyandot tribe also live in Kansas. According to the informative Wyandot Nation of Kansas website,

The Wyandot Nation of Kansas was incorporated in 1959 and is recognized by the State of Kansas as an Indian Tribe. The Wyandot Nation of Kansas is currently petitioning the U.S. Department of the Interior Bureau of Indian Affairs for federal recognition. The Wyandot Nation of Kansas is made up of those formerly known as "absentee" or "citizen class" Wyandot Indians. The Wyandot Nation of Kansas is dedicated to the preservation of Wyandot history and culture and the preservation, protection, restoration and maintenance of the Huron Indian Cemetery in Kansas City.[48]

Although the Huron and the Wyandot do not maintain formal contacts, they are still united by their common history as members of one of the most powerful Native American nations in North America.

The Sauk and Fox Tribe Today

Although the Sauk and Fox tribe has adopted many aspects of non–Native American culture, its members have remained a distinct community that has retained its unique traditions. Well into the twentieth century, most members of the tribe maintained their traditional culture, followed their religious beliefs, and spoke their native language.

In the late nineteenth century, the Sauk and Fox, who were once great farmers, were forced to relocate to Oklahoma, where the land was so poor that few could survive by relying on their ancient agricultural skills. By the beginning of the twentieth century, not a single Native American family was able to support itself by practicing commercial farming methods.

As a result, many Sauk and Fox tribespeople sold their land shares to white ranchers and farmers, who made a profit by farming large areas and tilling the land with expensive equipment. Without land to live on, Sauk and Fox people worked as laborers and ranch hands on the farms they themselves had once owned.

In 1912 oil was discovered on the remaining tribal land in Oklahoma, and the tribe members began to collectively receive about twenty-five thousand dollars a year from oil companies that drilled on their land. Despite this income, many Sauk and Fox tribespeople in Oklahoma lived in poverty. Today, most members of this tribe have relocated to nearby cities and towns.

There are still approximately one thousand Sauk and Fox members who live in central Iowa, where they were forced to move after Black Hawk's War. These tribespeople have maintained many aspects of their traditional culture. For example, they still practice ceremonies associated with sacred medicine.

Still, life for the Sauk and Fox is hard. Unemployment on the reservation remains high. In recent years it was 28 percent

Although most Native Americans have adopted aspects of modern culture, they still maintain their traditional cultures of ceremony and sacred medicine.

among the Sauk and Fox in Iowa and around 20 percent in Kansas. In Oklahoma the unemployment rate is as high as 59 percent. The lack of jobs has forced a majority of the Sauk and Fox to leave their reservations and seek employment elsewhere.

According to the 1990 U.S. Census, 4,700 Sauk and Fox live on the 15,072-acre Oklahoma reservation. About 564 Sauk and Fox tribespeople live on 3,300 acres of land on the Mesquakie reservation in Tama, Iowa. Forty-nine residents live on 80 acres of land on the Sauk and Fox reservation near the town of Reserve, Kansas, located on the Nebraska border.

Kansas is also home to other tribes who once lived along the Great Lakes. The Kickapoo reservation near Horton is home to 450 of the 1,500 Kickapoo Indians who live in Kansas. Meyetta, Kansas, is now home to 610 of the Potawatomi tribe. Another 3,500 Potawatomi live in nearby Topeka and the surrounding area.

The Ojibwa Today

Because the harsh climate made their lands less desirable to white settlers, the Ojibwa of northern Minnesota were the last of the Great Lakes tribes to be forced onto reservations. Their land was not ceded to the government until 1857, and

U.S. Army troops were still fighting minor skirmishes with Ojibwa at Leech Lake, Minnesota, as late as 1898.

Many of the Ojibwa living in Minnesota migrated there from northern Michigan and Wisconsin. In their isolated environment, they preserved the knowledge of the Midewiwin religion.

In the 1950s the Bureau of Indian Affairs instituted a program urging the

Jim Thorpe

Perhaps the most famous Sauk Indian of all time was the great athlete Jim Thorpe, who was born in Prague, Oklahoma, in 1888 and died in 1953. Thorpe played football at the Carlisle Indian School in Pennsylvania and was an All-American athlete in 1911 and 1912. While at Carlisle, he also played lacrosse (a game invented by Native Americans) and baseball and ran track. Thorpe set records in the 1912 Olympic Games while winning the decathlon and the pentathlon. In 1913 he was stripped of his gold medals, however, when it was learned that he had earned money playing baseball and was therefore not considered an amateur.

In 1915 Thorpe played professional football for the Canton, Ohio, Bulldogs. He later played for Marion and Toledo, both Ohio teams; Rock Island, Illinois; and New York. In addition, Thorpe played professional baseball from 1913 to 1919. In 1963, ten years after his death, he was made a charter member of the Pro Football Hall of Fame. In 1982, the International Olympic Committee voted to restore to Thorpe the medals it had taken from him nearly seventy years earlier.

Setting records in the 1912 Olympic Games, Jim Thorpe is perhaps the most famous Sauk Indian.

Ojibwa (and other tribes) to leave their reservations and migrate to urban areas. By the mid-1970s over 12,000 of Minnesota's 22,322 Native Americans had moved to cities such as Minneapolis, St. Paul, and Duluth, as well as Chicago, Illinois, and Denver, Colorado. Although these relocations might have helped some Native Americans to find jobs, the cost in terms of lost culture was high.

Starting in the 1960s, Native Americans living in St. Paul established alternative schools and offered native language classes to students. Tribal councils on reservations provided scholarships for hundreds of high school students to attend universities and trade schools. In the 1970s the state of Minnesota appropriated hundreds of thousands of dollars to establish Native American college scholarships. The University of Minnesota established the Department of American Indian Studies, which provided counselors, tutors, and instruction in Ojibwa and Sioux languages. Other colleges in Wisconsin and Michigan also promote similar programs.

As a result of these programs, Ojibwa high school and college dropout rates declined significantly. In addition, these programs have generated increased pride in education and in Ojibwa culture.

Several Ojibwa authors have won literary and public service awards for their work detailing modern tribal life. Maude Kegg, born in 1902, was one of the dwindling number of Minnesotans still able to speak fluent Ojibwa. She wrote and contributed to many books about Ojibwa language and traditions. Kegg was given the National Heritage Fellowship Award by President George Bush in 1990. She died in 1996.

Gerald Vizenor, a member of the Minnesota Ojibwa tribe, has been honored with the New York Fiction Collective Prize, an American Book Award, the PEN Oakland, and an artists fellowship in literature from the California Arts Council.

Today, approximately two hundred thousand members of the Ojibwa tribe are widely dispersed in various communities, mostly in the Midwest. They live on more than one hundred reservations in Michigan, Wisconsin, Minnesota, North Dakota, and Montana as well as the Canadian provinces of Ontario, Manitoba, and Saskatchewan. The Ojibwa belong to fifteen federally recognized tribal organizations. Three more Ojibwa-Ottawa bands are currently seeking federal acknowledgment. About seventy bands have been granted federal status in Canada.

Native American Casinos

Without a doubt, the most important change to come on Native American reservations in the twentieth century has been the introduction of so-called Indian gaming, or casino-style gambling, which was legalized in the 1980s. The money generated from these casinos is allowing at least some tribal governments to reverse the effects of three centuries of poverty and federal neglect on reservations.

Since tribal land has always been a legal entity separate from the United States, the federal and state governments, technically at least, had no right to outlaw gambling on reservations. Large-scale gaming sponsored by tribal governments began in 1988 with the passage of the Indian Gaming Regulatory Act (IGRA). With this law, the U.S. Congress formally recognized the right of Native Americans to conduct gaming operations on their sovereign lands.

Native Americans immediately began construction of Las Vegas–style gambling casinos on their lands. Those casinos located near larger cities and towns became very popular and generated huge revenues for tribes in a way that no federal stimulus ever had before.

After decades of poverty and high unemployment, Native Americans began to see gaming as an important part of their tribal economies and as a way to gain self-sufficiency. The right of Native Americans to sponsor gaming has not gone unchallenged, however, and resistance from the state governments and private gaming interests still threatens Native American casino operations.

As of February 1997, there were 115 tribes with gambling operations in twenty-four states. Several of the most successful casinos are operated by Native Americans of the Great Lakes region. According to the National Indian Gaming Association, Wisconsin tribes operate fifteen gaming facilities with a total payroll of just over $68 million. Of the more than forty-five hundred people employed by tribal gaming operations, two thousand are non–Native American. One-half of the forty-

five hundred casino employees were previously unemployed, and 20 percent were receiving welfare. If those same employees were placed on state unemployment compensation, it would cost the state more than $27 million.

Taken together, Native American casinos are Minnesota's seventh largest employer, having created nearly ten thousand jobs, 75 percent of which are held by non–Native Americans. Minnesota's seventeen tribal casinos generated revenues of $390 million in 1992. That year Minnesota casinos paid more than $37 million in state and federal payroll taxes and benefits.

Michigan tribes operate eight gaming operations and employ two thousand people, nearly 40 percent of whom are non–Native American. Payrolls at Michigan casinos are estimated at $13.5 million annually. Prior to taking casino jobs, approximately 37 percent of tribal gaming employees were receiving state or federal welfare assistance and an additional 31 percent were receiving state or federal unemployment compensation.

Although some people believe that Indian gaming has made average Native Americans rich, tribes are utilizing most of the profits to pay off costs incurred to enable them to go into gaming, such as building casinos, hotels, restaurants, and roads. The rest of the money is going toward building self-sufficiency and government infrastructure on reservations. Since IGRA allows only the tribal governments to enter into gaming (not individuals), the tribes are using their gaming profits for

Powwows

Powwows are community gatherings in which Native Americans come together to share songs and dances and celebrate their language, heritage, and culture. During the last twenty years, powwows have become part of a popular culture shared by many Native American nations.

Powwows bring together the dances, songs, and oral traditions of several Algonquian and western Native American tribes. Some of these traditions are centuries old. In the Great Lakes area, powwows were held only occasionally during the early twentieth century. The Grand River powwow at Six Nations reservation, an Iroquoian community, has been celebrated each July for decades. The Ann Arbor powwow in Michigan has been taking place since 1975. Powwows are open to everyone, Native American and non–Native American alike.

At a powwow, there is a central open space for dancers and singers. The event is usually opened by an elder speaking in a native language. Members of a drum circle make music for the event. Dancers in beautiful costumes sometimes dance together or participate in competitions featuring many different dance styles. The Powwow Home Page describes the modern events.

"Powwows are weekend events, usually celebrated from mid March through early September. A powwow lasts 2 or 3 days, getting underway by mid-morning and ending in the evening. During the last 20 years, the number of powwows held across North America has increased dramatically. They're held at arenas, recreation buildings, fair grounds and traditional sites in urban centers or Native reserves, from Florida to California, from British Columbia to New Brunswick—the four corners of Turtle Island."

Traditionally, an elder speaker signified the beginning of a powwow.

law enforcement, education, economic development, tribal courts, and infrastructure improvement such as building houses, schools, roads, and sewer and water systems. This money also benefits individuals by funding social service programs, scholarships, health care clinics, and chemical dependency treatment programs.

Less than one-third of the 557 Native American tribes in the United States have benefited from Indian gaming, however. The rest are still struggling to lift themselves out of a centuries-old cycle of poverty. Tribes in rural areas of Oklahoma, Iowa, North Dakota, and elsewhere are too removed from population centers to operate successful casinos. It remains to be seen, then, whether gaming will prove to be the economic savior of Native Americans as a group.

Indian Games and Gambling

Indian gaming was originally a part of tribal ceremonies or celebrations and existed long before Europeans came to America. Native American men and women made dicelike gambling instruments from peach pits, and they also bet on foot races, archery, javelin throwing, and other endurance contests as well as horse races. Olympic-style games were often played between villages and members of other tribes. The details of Native American games were revealed in Lewis Henry Morgan's *League of the Ho-de-no-sau-nee or Iroquois.*

"In their national games is to be found another fruitful source of amusement in Indian life. These games were not only played at religious festivals, at which they often formed a conspicuous part of the entertainment, but special days were frequently set apart for their celebrations.

They entered into these diversions with the highest zeal . . . and took unwearied pains to perfect themselves in the art of playing each successfully. There were but six principal games among the Iroquois, and these are divisible into athletic games, and games of chance. . . .

Betting on the result [of sporting events] was common among the Iroquois. As this practice was never reprobated by their religious teachers, but, on the contrary, rather encouraged, it frequently led to the most reckless indulgence. It often happened that the Indian gambled away every valuable article which he possessed; his tomahawk, his medal, his ornaments, and even his blanket. . . .

These bets were made in a systematic manner, and the articles then deposited with the managers of the game. . . . Personal ornaments were the usual gaming currency . . . until hundreds of articles were sometimes collected."

In spite of the changes over the years, Native Americans continue to honor ancient traditions and rituals such as the gathering of maple syrup from the sugarbush.

Native Traditions in the Twenty-First Century

Neon-flashing Native American casinos are just one of the many aspects of the Great Lakes region that have changed radically over the past three hundred years. Roads, factories, strip malls, cities, and suburbs dominate the landscape where the Iroquois and Ojibwa once hunted in a boundless forest wilderness. Much like U.S. citizens whose relatives once came from Italy, Africa, Mexico, or France, today's Native Americans find themselves in a world much different from that of their ancestors.

In spite of all these changes, many of today's Native Americans still venture out on lakes and rivers in canoes to fish and collect wild rice. City dwellers rejoin their friends and families on the reservations for such occasions. The first grains of wild rice are still offered to the spirits in a first-fruit ceremony. Maple syrup is still collected from sugarbush, and annual sugaring rituals are still conducted under the cold spring moon.

Although to some extent they have assimilated into the larger American culture, the ancient spirit of the people of the lakes persists whenever they come together to honor their traditions of peace and power.

Notes

Introduction: An Ancient Odyssey

1. Luther Standing Bear, *Land of the Spotted Eagle.* 1933. Reprint, Lincoln, NE: Bison Book Printing, 1978, pp. 227–28.
2. Edna L. Paisano, *We, the First Americans,* U.S. Census Bureau, 1993, p. 1. www.census.gov/apsd/wepeople/we-5.pdf.

Chapter 1: Native Peoples of the Great Lakes

3. Lewis Henry Morgan, *League of the Ho-de-no-sau-nee or Iroquois.* 1851. Reprint, New York: Citadel Press, 1993, p. 3.
4. Alvin M. Josephy Jr., *500 Nations.* New York: Alfred A. Knopf, 1994, p. 48.
5. Josephy, *500 Nations,* p. 50.
6. Cadwallader Colden, *The History of the Five Nations of Canada,* vol. 1. New York: Allerton Books, 1922, p. xvii.
7. Josephy, *500 Nations,* p. 53.
8. George Irving Quimby, *Indian Life in the Upper Great Lakes.* Chicago: University of Chicago Press, 1960, p. 108.

Chapter 2: Lodges of the Great Lakes Clans

9. James A. Maxwell, ed., *America's Fascinating Indian Heritage.* Pleasantville, NY: Reader's Digest Associates, 1978, p. 111.

10. Morgan, *League of the Ho-de-no-sau-nee or Iroquois,* p. 314.
11. Quoted in Charles Johnson, ed., *The Valley of the Six Nations.* Toronto: University of Toronto Press, 1964, p. 24.
12. Morgan, *League of the Ho-de-no-sau-nee or Iroquois,* p. 314.
13. Quoted in Johnson, *The Valley of the Six Nations,* p. 25.
14. Morgan, *League of the Ho-de-no-sau-nee or Iroquois,* p. 318.
15. Maxwell, *America's Fascinating Indian Heritage,* p. 124.
16. Quoted in Emma Helen Blair, ed., *The Indian Tribes of the Upper Mississippi Valley and Region of the Great Lakes.* 1911. Reprint, Lincoln: University of Nebraska Press, 1996, pp. 228–29.
17. Quimby, *Indian Life in the Upper Great Lakes,* p. 129.
18. Quimby, *Indian Life in the Upper Great Lakes,* p. 116.
19. Quoted in Mary Inez Hilger, *Chippewa Child Life.* 1951. Reprint, St. Paul: Minnesota Historical Society, 1992, p. 154.
20. Quoted in Hilger, *Chippewa Child Life,* p. 157.
21. Quoted in Hilger, *Chippewa Child Life,* p. 159.

22. Quoted in Blair, *The Indian Tribes of the Upper Mississippi Valley and Region of the Great Lakes,* p. 167.

Chapter 3: The Bounty of the Four Seasons

23. Editors of Time-Life Books, *People of the Lakes.* Alexandria, VA: Time-Life Books, 1994, p. 17.
24. Hilger, *Chippewa Child Life,* p. 125.
25. Quoted in Blair, *The Indian Tribes of the Upper Mississippi Valley and Region of the Great Lakes,* p. 304.
26. Morgan, *League of the Ho-de-no-sau-nee or Iroquois,* p. 370.
27. Morgan, *League of the Ho-de-no-sau-nee or Iroquois,* p. 319.
28. Maxwell, *America's Fascinating Indian Heritage,* p. 124.
29. Morgan, *League of the Ho-de-no-sau-nee or Iroquois,* p. 377.
30. Editors of Time-Life Books, *People of the Lakes,* p. 51.

Chapter 4: Spirits and Healing

31. Morgan, *League of the Ho-de-no-sau-nee or Iroquois,* pp. 154–55.
32. Morgan, *League of the Ho-de-no-sau-nee or Iroquois,* pp. 157–58.
33. Cottie Burland, *North American Indian Mythology,* rev. ed. New York: Peter Bedrick Books, 1985, p. 64.
34. Editors of Time-Life Books, *People of the Lakes,* pp. 87–88.
35. Hilger, *Chippewa Child Life,* p. 35.
36. Editors of Time-Life Books, *People of the Lakes,* p. 87.
37. Quoted in Hilger, *Chippewa Child Life,* p. 41.
38. Quoted in Hilger, *Chippewa Child Life,* p. 42.
39. Hilger, *Chippewa Child Life,* pp. 41–42.
40. Quimby, *Indian Life in the Upper Great Lakes,* p. 119.
41. Quimby, *Indian Life in the Upper Great Lakes,* pp. 120–21.

Chapter 5: War and Conflict

42. Maxwell, *America's Fascinating Indian Heritage,* p. 149.
43. Editors of Time-Life Books, *Realm of the Iroquois.* Alexandria, VA: Time-Life Books, 1993, p. 55.
44. Black Hawk, *Black Hawk: An Autobiography.* Ed. Donald Jackson. Urbana: University of Illinois Press, 1955, p. 115.
45. Black Hawk, *Black Hawk,* pp. 164–65.

Chapter 6: People of the Lakes Today

46. Edna L. Paisano, "The American Indian, Eskimo, and Aleut Population," U.S. Census Bureau, January 29, 1999. www.census.gov/population/www/pop-profile/amerind.html.
47. National Indian Gaming Association, "Where the Proceeds Go." www.indiangaming.org/proceeds.html.
48. Wyandot Nation of Kansas, July 7, 1998. http://history.cc.ukans.edu/kansas/wn/wn_main.html.

For Further Reading

Books

Black Hawk, *Black Hawk: An Autobiography.* Ed. Donald Jackson. Urbana: University of Illinois Press, 1955. First published in 1833, this book is the life story of Sauk chief Black Hawk. It is a valuable resource that details the Native American view of the so-called Black Hawk's War, the events that led to it, and the wise Native American's view of the white society that invaded his ancestral homeland.

Cottie Burland, *North American Indian Mythology.* Rev. ed. New York: Peter Bedrick Books, 1985. This book explores the rich heritage of tribal religious beliefs from the fishermen of the Pacific Northwest to the tribes of the Great Lakes. It discusses the deities and heroes, mythical figures, spirits, and medicine men of dozens of tribes.

Samuel de Champlain, *Voyages of Samuel de Champlain 1604–1618.* 1907. Reprint, New York: Barnes & Noble, 1946. In his diary, Champlain recounts his exploration of the Iroquois country in the 1600s, before the land had been changed by white people. It is an important work of history that helps the reader understand the clash of cultures between the Europeans and the Native Americans.

James Clifton, *The Potawatomi.* New York: Chelsea House, 1987. A book in the Indians of North America series, this one explores the details of the Potawatomi.

Editors of Time-Life Books, *People of the Lakes.* Alexandria, VA: Time-Life Books, 1994. Another beautiful book from the editors of Time-Life, this one uses fascinating facts, well-researched text, photos, and drawings to bring alive the culture of the Ojibwa, Kickapoo, Ottawa, Potawatomi, and other Great Lakes tribes.

Editors of Time-Life Books, *Realm of the Iroquois*. Alexandria, VA: Time-Life Books, 1993. A fascinating and informative book about the Iroquois tribes, illustrated with dozens of photographs, maps, and drawings.

Lewis Henry Morgan, *League of the Ho-de-no-sau-nee or Iroquois*. 1851. Reprint, New York: Citadel Press, 1993. Morgan's book was one of the few nineteenth-century books that respectfully discussed Native Americans. In Morgan's own words, he wrote the book "to encourage a kinder feeling towards the Indian, founded upon a truer knowledge of his civil and domestic institutions." The book offers detailed explanations of Iroquois daily life and traditions as seen through the eyes of a white American.

Patricia K. Ourada, *The Menominee*. New York: Chelsea House, 1990. A book providing detailed information about Menominee culture and history from the Indians of North America series.

Luther Standing Bear, *Land of the Spotted Eagle*. 1933. Reprint, Lincoln, NE: Bison Book Printing, 1978. Standing Bear was a Lakota Sioux born in the mid-1860s. He wrote this book in 1933 to tell white people how the traditional Lakota lived. The book is full of personal reminiscences and includes chapters on child rearing, social organization of the Lakota, and Native American religion. Standing Bear has many harsh words for the baffling behavior and hypocrisy of the white people who subjugated his people.

Helen Hornbeck Tanner, *The Ojibwa*. New York: Chelsea House, 1992. A book rich with detailed information about Ojibwa culture and history from the Indians of North America series.

Helen Hornbeck Tanner, ed., *Atlas of Great Lakes Indian History*. Norman: University of Oklahoma Press, 1987. This atlas helps clarify the history of the Great Lakes tribes through the use of thirty-three maps and accompanying text. It graphically displays the movement of Native American communities from 1640 to 1871, and it also shows intertribal warfare, disease epidemics, trade routes, and land cessions. It is a good visual aid to understanding the history of the people of the lakes.

Carl Waldman, *Encyclopedia of Native American Tribes.* New York: Facts On File, 1988. A comprehensive reference work that covers more than 150 tribes of North America. Organized alphabetically by tribe, it accesses locations, migrations, contacts with whites, wars, and present-day tribal affairs.

Websites

Index of Native American Resources on the Internet (www. hanksville.org/NAresources/). This index has links to pages concerning Native American culture, history, education, language, health, indigenous knowledge, art, galleries, and genealogy.

Iroquois Information Links (http://tuscaroras.com/pages/irlinks_ na.html). This page has links to many sites maintained by members of the Iroquois Nation.

Oneida Indian Nation (http://one-web.org/oneida/). One of the original members of the Iroquois League, the Oneida enjoy a unique role in American history because their tribe supported the colonists in their struggle for independence from England. The nation exists as a sovereign political unit, which predates the U.S. Constitution.

Powwow Home Page (www.si.umich.edu/CHICO/MHN/powwow_ new/questions/question_frame.html). This page has complete information about Native American powwows and links to powwow sites and schedules.

Seneca Nation of Indians (http://members.localnet.com/~sni/). The home page of the Seneca Nation of Indians, one of the six tribes of the Iroquois League that occupies aboriginal lands in New York State set aside by the 1794 Treaty of Canandaigua. The Seneca Nation has a total population of over sixty-seven hundred enrolled members.

Six Nations of the Grand River Reservation in Canada (www.geocities.com/Athens/Olympus/3808/). This page has dozens of links to Iroquois-related sites, including the *Turtle Island News,* a weekly periodical featuring news of the Six Nations.

Twin Groves Junior High School of Buffalo Grove, Illinois (www.twingroves.district96.k12.il.us/NativeAmericans/Tribes%

26Nations.html). A well-researched and comprehensive website with links to dozens of other sites maintained by Native American tribes. The links feature literature by tribal members as well as historical and native language information.

Wyandot Nation of Kansas (http://history.cc.ukans.edu/kansas/wn/wn_main.html). The Wyandot are also known as the Huron, and they were forced to move from Canada to Kansas. This incredibly comprehensive page includes the history of the Wyandot, sacred sites, treaties, language, literature, links, and more.

Works Consulted

Books

Emma Helen Blair, ed., *The Indian Tribes of the Upper Mississippi Valley and Region of the Great Lakes.* 1911. Reprint, Lincoln: University of Nebraska Press, 1996. This book is a collection of essays from army officers, Indian agents, and missionaries who described Native Americans of the upper Great Lakes region between 1716 and 1820. Although the writers were obviously prejudiced against their subjects, the book offers insight into Native American culture before it was radically changed by white people.

Cadwallader Colden, *The History of the Five Nations of Canada.* Vol. 1. New York: Allerton Books, 1922. This book is a fascinating discussion of Iroquois wars, trade with the English, treaties, and customs.

Editors of Time-Life Books, *The Reservations.* Alexandria, VA: Time-Life Books, 1995. A book about Native American history and culture after the tribes were ordered onto reservations. Many color pictures and maps illustrate the easy-to-understand text.

Mary Inez Hilger, *Chippewa Child Life.* 1951. Reprint, St. Paul: Minnesota Historical Society, 1992. In the 1930s, anthropologist Mary Inez Hilger traveled to nine reservations in Minnesota, Wisconsin, and Michigan to record Ojibwa child-rearing methods. This book details her findings and also gives a comprehensive overview of Ojibwa culture as gleaned from those on the reservations old enough to remember the old ways before the white people arrived.

Charles Johnson, ed., *The Valley of the Six Nations.* Toronto: University of Toronto Press, 1964. Published for the government of Ontario, this book consists of documents related to the Indian lands along the Grand River. The book offers many quotes from early European explorers as well as mind-numbing details from treaties and contracts that demonstrate how difficult these treaties were to understand, even to those who understood English.

Alvin M. Josephy Jr., *500 Nations*. New York: Alfred A. Knopf, 1994. This superbly written book by a celebrated historian details the entire history of Native Americans from the earliest years, when mastodons roamed the earth, to the last battles and life on the reservations. Lavishly illustrated with paintings, woodcuts, drawings, photos, and Native American artifacts, this book gives a detailed overview of America's five hundred Indian nations.

James A. Maxwell, ed., *America's Fascinating Indian Heritage*. Pleasantville, NY: Reader's Digest Associates, 1978. A book that explores the first Americans, their customs, art, history, and how they lived. It is illustrated with dozens of drawings, photos, and other informative media.

George Irving Quimby, *Indian Life in the Upper Great Lakes*. Chicago: University of Chicago Press, 1960. A scholarly work by an anthropologist, this book details the lives and history of the tribes in the northwestern Great Lakes region from ancient times to the breakdown of the culture under American pressure in the 1820s.

Henry Rowe Schoolcraft, *Travels Through the Northwest Regions of the U.S.* 1821. Reprint, Ann Arbor, MI: University Microfilms, 1966. This book chronicles Schoolcraft's journeys around the southern shores of Lake Superior as well as along the Mississippi River in Minnesota. Written for the U.S. government, the book was meant to show that the United States could subdue the Native Americans and support a considerable population of settlers.

Veronica E. Tiller, ed., *Discover Reservations USA: A Visitor's Welcome Guide*. Denver: Council, 1992. This book is the only guide sanctioned by Native American tribes for travelers wishing to visit Indian reservations. The book lists the size and population of every reservation in the United States along with the commercial activities found on each, including arts and crafts stores, bingo parlors, and gaming casinos. It gives detailed maps and addresses to all reservations as well as campgrounds and archaeological and historic sites.

Internet Sources

Edna L. Paisano, "The American Indian, Eskimo, and Aleut Population," U.S. Census Bureau, January 29, 1999. www.census.gov/population/www/pop-profile/amerind.html.

————, *We, the First Americans,* U.S. Census Bureau, 1993. www.census.gov/apsd/wepeople/we-5.pdf. Published on the Internet by the U.S. Census Bureau, this article details specific economic and population statistics about Native Americans living the United States today.

National Indian Gaming Association, "Where the Proceeds Go." www.indiangaming.org/proceeds.html. The web page for the National Indian Gaming Association represents over 150 sovereign Indian nations interested in preserving Native American sovereignty and protecting their rights in tribal gaming and other enterprises. NIGA provides information about the history of Indian gaming, statistics on gaming, how gaming proceeds are spent, and a wealth of information on Native American issues.

Index

Picture Credits

Cover photo: Corbis
Archive Photos, 45, 79, 86, 88, 91, 95
Cumberland County Historical Society, 92
Dover Publications, 76
Library of Congress, 11, 21, 24, 36, 58, 61, 71, 73, 77, 80, 81
North Wind, 14, 17, 18, 28, 37, 42, 47, 51, 57, 75, 97
Planet Art, 63
Stock Montage, Inc., 30, 33, 41, 49, 54, 78

About the Author

Stuart A. Kallen is the author of more than 145 nonfiction books for children and young adults. He has written on topics ranging from the theory of relativity to rock-and-roll history to life on the American frontier. In addition, Mr. Kallen has written award-winning children's videos and television scripts. In his spare time, Stuart A. Kallen is a singer/songwriter/guitarist in San Diego, California.